Whispered Shadows

A Poetry Anthology

Beverly L. Anderson

Phoenix Voices Publishing

Contents

Prologue

Whispered Shadows of My Mind

Twisting and turning paths make their way through the emptiness. This place cannot be found on a map, so no one bothers to look. I found my way, but now I'm lost. I am trapped in a self-made world. While others may find this circumstance troublesome, I do not. I don't belong in this world. I cannot live in the world that most consider reality. The shadows mold and shift around me. They whisper in my mind eternally. Twisting and turning in an infinite series of corridors and alleys, this place spirals around me.

Lost. I use that word, but considering this is a shadow of my mind, can that be true? No, not in reality. Something in my mind illuminates the things I write. Within the shadows, a wellspring emerges, giving birth to ideas and thoughts longing to be seen. Is this hubris on my part? Is it egotism? Some argue that writers are egotistical as they seek visibility and admiration. The writer, on the whole, desires to touch someone's heart in reality. We are driven not by a desire for fame or fortune. It's not about egotism or pride. The words we express hold magic, and poetry embodies that magic in its purest form. It is pure, devoid of dialogue, excessive explanations, or unnecessary words.

I was once told that poetry was a dead form of writing. This person said to me that no one reads poetry anymore, and there's no place for it in our technologically advanced world. She thought it was old, stiff, and boring. I disagree. I find poetry to be one of the most enduring forms of writing. The reasoning is simple. A poem has no time frame. While a novel is bound to a specific time and setting, a poem offers the freedom to be transplanted to another situation and reinterpreted. Today, we can still read and apply the works of Alfred Lord Tennyson and Samuel Taylor Coleridge to our society. We can use Shakespeare and Lord Byron's poetry in this time to capture the intended emotions. Poetry outlasts other literature. The short form of poetry embodies an eternal nature. Something so succinct and simple yet infinitely complex at the exact moment. Even a haiku of 5-7-5 speaks volumes about the poet's vision in their mind.

Come and step into my world, where you will find poetry that I have written throughout my life, from my middle and high school years until I published this volume. Some are very simple, others are more complex. Some show rudimentary skills, others much more developed skills. The change and the evolution of my writing over time are almost tangible, and I feel like it reflects the very nature of the shadows that swirl within my consciousness. Find meaning in these poems and savor a cup of tea while you do. I recommend a nice chai.

PART ONE

Whispered Fantasy

In between the worlds lies a place where we escape. Fantasy is not only a place for fantastical creatures such as unicorns, fairies, mermaids, elves, monsters, and dragons. It is a place where more mundane dreams and hopes live. The future holds uncertain things for all of us, and we find ourselves entranced by daydreams that contain our fondest hopes and ideals. Fantasy holds different things for everyone. Dreams are something that keep us heading forward. The word fantasy conjures images of elves, dwarves, and magical spells, but in reality, fantasy is anything you can imagine. Everyone fantasizes about different things, from having a large family to living a quiet retirement out in a tropical location. Dreams and wishes fill our minds throughout our lives, from the simplest childhood dream of a toy to our grown-up desires for that perfect job. Out of that desire and dream comes the drive to live our lives and strive for better and bigger things. We dream, we wish, we desire, and we strive. Combine those things, and we, as a species, can achieve anything we set our minds to.

To make those fantasies a reality, one more thing is required: creativity. Creativity springs from our imagination and desire to make fantasy a reality. Someone dreamed up things like mobile phones, tablet computers, and every invention we have today. Where would we be without imagination and willingness to delve into our fantasies? Science fiction grows and becomes a science fact, and the world constantly shifts and changes. Does fantasy truly imply impossibility, or does it merely denote improbability and difficulty in attainment?

Are we likely to encounter a sword and sorcery world with magic and beauty like we've never seen? Science seems like magic to those who do not understand it. The people in the Middle Ages would burn a person from today as a witch or worship them as a god if they appeared with wristwatches, mobile phones, and other gadgets. Understanding the unknown makes it more manageable. Today, radio waves hold no significance, but in the past, the concept of invisible sound waves emanating from a box was so unfamiliar that it evoked fear.

Genetic mutations are possible, and so we wonder, will mutants one day exist like they do in comic books? Can superpowers really become real? Do vampires stalk the night? Is there somewhere that a blue box will materialize and quietly save the world? We don't know those answers for certain, so we keep searching, in our imaginations and in the world.

How do we know exactly what we will discover? So now step into my fantasy and see where they lead you. You'll find surreal things, beautiful things, horrible things, and just plain unknown things. They are the emotions that have occupied my mind for years. Perhaps you will find yourself drawn to one or more of the concepts I've presented. I hope so. Open yourself to the possibilities that you may not have realized existed before.

A Vampire's Beginning

He was a young man.
She was a young
woman.
They were in love.

A dark night came, one
with no moon.
He went out for a walk
alone.
At an end his thoughts
would be soon.
Through the darkness,
he heard a moan.

He turned and looked
behind of him.
He saw a girl upon the
ground.
And then all the lights
went dim.
Now, he knew what girl
he had found.

He stumbled away, and
he knew.
His life as a man was
over.
Though he did not
know what to do,
He did know that all was

over.

Then he went to his
love, that night.
He told her what he had
become.
And she wanted to make
it right.|
She beckoned him to
with her come.

Brave, she told him she
was ready.
He was afraid of what he
was,
She held him and she
was steady.
He knew exactly what
he was.

She smiled and said now
they could be
really together forever,
Before long though she
could not see.
And she'd be with her
love never.

He was a young man.
She was a young
woman.
They were in love.

Battle

My heart burns fire in
my chest.
My blood traces fire in
my veins.
My eyes burn within my
face.
My lungs breath fire.
My breath comes fast.
And battle begins.

The heat of battle,
The fever of combat.
The passion of the fight.
Knives, guns, swords, or
bare hands,
Instruments of destruc-
tion and pain all.
Hard steel meeting soft
flesh.
Blood spilling painting
the soil crimson.

The fight begins,
And it brings the fever.
My blood rushes, burn-
ing my body.
My muscles strain, try-
ing to keep me alive,
Just a moment longer.
My heart pumping
faster, keeping me alive.

To live is the challenge in
battle.
I will win to fight again.
I live for fighting, I live
for battle.
I search for wars, and I
find them.
I live for the sound of my
heart pounding in my
ears.
I edge closer to my very
mortality.
I thrill for being so close
to death.
It invigorates me to fight
and win.
To feel fire in my heart
and my blood burning
with strength.
To live and fight again
another day.

On the Funeral Pyre

The dead have been
piled here today,
the flames of the pyre
burn up towards the sky,
and there is nothing that
we can do at all
as we that remain here
watch it burn high.

The bodies are not what
matter anymore,
as the souls within them
are long gone.
they have been taken
away from this world of
pain,
and you should not
weep too long for them.

Evil men do evil deeds,
and this is true,
but all you can do is be
good people in this face
and try to take on your
life without evil
and you will have no
true pain any more.

Forget what you have
seen dear ones,
forget the violence, with

which they died,
and remember the lives,
which they lived.
keep this in mind
though it is hard to do.

There is hurt and there
is much anger
against those that have
brought death
here to your once peace-
ful lands
but do not think on it
like that.

They would not see you
fret with worried faces,
they would see you
stand and be true.
Despite the death that
has been piled all around
you,
remember that this is
not all there is to our life.

The actions of one man
can bring about the
downfall
of all that live together in
one single place,
and bring the death
of thousands to your
doors.
this is something that I
fear cannot be changed.

Mercy is above all what
they have not,
to slay the living with
such fervor as we have
seen here.
this sweet land, you are
not alone in this all,
I feel your suffering and
your sorrow today.

Here stand with me
somewhere safe for a
moment,
in between the world of
light and darkness.
there is a shadow of pain
across you all right now,
but remember the light
and dark that is around
you.

The light is the mercy,
the hope, and the love
that you need right now,
that they would want.
The dark is the hate, the
anger, and the revenge
that you do not need,
that they would not
want.

The shadow of pain, the
shadow of fear,
it is of the unknown,

and no more.
The shadow is cast by
those in the light,
the shadow is cast into
the dark.

Do not fear this shadow
my dear friends.
It is because of the light
that it has formed.
Cast away your dark-
ness, and come to the
light.
life ends as it begins,
with blood and pain.

Those that have died
are now gone from this
world,
but they have traveled
on to the next one.

Seduction in White

Vision in white,
she floats towards me
like
a silent image of my
soul...

Are you an angel
or a demon
or are you simply a re-
flection?

Eyes flutter
in the darkness
as the image
becomes one
with me.

How do I speak?
How do I learn?

Am I sleeping?
Or am I finally awake?

I don't know,
I lost the ability to rea-
son
Long ago.

Silent arms encircling
and I'm choking
on a mist

but I'm so comfortable
here
I don't want to fight...

Ah, to answer my ques-
tion,
now I know what you
are,
and I've slipped into
your seduction
willfully.

Unreal Fantasies

A fantasy of some sort
builds its vision in my
mind.

What does it mean?
Is it something real?
Touch the ending,
and touch the begin-
ning...

where does the fantasy
end
and the reality begin
if it even does ever end

I'm caught forever
it seems
somewhere   I   don't
know
how to escape.

I need the fantasy to sur-
vive,
inside my mind,
nothing else matters
but what is unreal...

or is any of it unreal?

My Own Way

I could not live the way
they said,
I only wanted to choose
my own way,
And they would not let
me.
They said I was wrong
to want my freedom.
They said their way was
the only way.
I did not agree with
them,
So I decided to find my
own way.
I am leaving them far
behind,
And I am finding my
own way.
And though they will
not admit it,
Many others have done
the same.
Now I search for those
who have left before,
And I will join them
when I find them.
I will have my freedom,
One way or another.
I will not live without it.
I have lived under the
iron hand of tyranny,

And I will never live
there again.
I have grabbed onto
freedom with both
hands,
And I will never let it go.
I see a campfire in the
distance,
And in it, I see a future
for me,
My own way.

Ballad of the Dancers
in Shadow

The world of ours has
been so changed and
warped
By the battles of the ti-
tans and divine.
The light of hope and
goodness is so dim,
But there are those that
strive to see the sign.

There are those that
fight the evil of the ti-
tans,
Slayers of their harmful
spawn, they do good
But know some can
change and become di-
vine
In this world wounded
by the evil blood.

But what of love in this
hurt, pained world?
Love of a lover mated at
the very soul?
What of the kind of love
for someone pure
Untainted, innocent as a
deer's foal?

Bound by the blood of
magic to start,
Two people fated to love
each other
would find their love
through the shadow
in which they danced,
not knowing one an-
other.

Both danced the place in
between, the border
Between   complete
darkness and utter light.
They had none but the
shadow to hold to
When standing against
forces of eternal night.

To become the Queen of
the Dead was what
The wight lord wished
the sorceress to become.
A remnant of the once
great high elves old,
He wished her to create
a new race of some.

He thought he had her
friends dead and gone,
But a mystery began he
had not known of.
A gentle thief from the
city and two more
Rescued her friends,

and so begins our tale of
love.

He'd fallen in love with
the elf from afar,
And was sent to where
she was to aid her
To know prayers are
heard very often
And answers give to
those pious and sure.

The search began for
their dear friend,
And they found their
way into his realm of the
dead.
They found her in great
pain and distress.
They took her to dwar-
ven hold, as they were
led.

Her eyes were vacant
and they wondered
If she would ever come
back to real life
As she once was before
all this came to be,
Before her soul was cut
deeply with the knife.

The thief took his
chance with his love
soon,

And went to her in the
night, and in the dark,
To tell her of his faith
and love in her,
And silently he hoped
he made a mark.

The pain was too much
for the thief to pierce,
But he did what he
could and became a
friend.
Which, truth be known
was what she needed,
While she waited for her
broken spirit to mend.

The dance of shadows
came to her very soon,
And away they went to
the Shadow plane
To rescue a friend there
kept in prison,
They found there,
nothing was the same.

Though the sorceress
found even there
Her past came about to
haunt her life.
And the Lady of
Vengeance came nigh
And asked them all of
the pain and strife.

The sorceress held to her
ideals and goddess,
And did not fall to the
emotions she felt.
She was determined to
move on with it,
Even though a hard
hand she was dealt.

The one that turned her
on the path
They rescued from a
shadow lord.
And back they came to
dwarven hold,
And once more took up
spell and sword.

There was no time for
her to heal,
And there was no time
for him to try,
So away they went to
fight the undead,
And the thief had to
wait by and by.

Time passed, and the elf
returned to him,
But still there was the
sadness in her eyes.
Then marched the
armies on the citadel,
And they had to discern
truth from lies.

It seemed the undead
lord who held her
Had taken more from
her than they knew,
And had also deemed to
arrange for
Her to, in the heat of the
battle, something do.

A fell ritual brought the
brave sorceress out,
And into the ring, on
her knees she fell.
Without knowing the
cause, a crooning voice
From her called forth
children like a bell.

Then before her eyes
stood all that she feared,
And beside him a crea-
ture of her flesh he'd
made,
A vision of terror, half of
her, half of him,
Her heart stopped in the
midst of this raid.

It seemed her escape
with her friends was
false,
For it was deemed to re-
turn her to this place
So that the undead lord

might have the children
Or the surrender of the
dwarves in face.

Then, the shining light
of the great gods,
Put an end to the suffer-
ing of the dwarves here,
And the armies were
forced to leave,
But the elf still shook
with fear.

To return to her, her
lord had sworn,
As he walked away with
her child.
And all she could do was
wonder when,
Her heart with filled of
fear and eyes wild.

Time stopped for the
lovers fated to naught,
Until our thief went to
her once more in night.
He held her through the
tears and grief,
And pushed back the
darkness with all his
might.

Love, after all, is a
salve to cure the deepest
wound,

And all he could do was
give all he had to her.
She was wounded very
deep, but she realized,
Her soul had awoken
with him finally at his
lure.

Those that dance in
shadows dance still to-
day,
The sorceress still some-
what wounded and sad,
But with the thief to
dance by her side,
She had come to realize
that it will not be so bad.

Swift in the patronage of
the gods,
Still they find those who
need their aid,
And dance softly in be-
tween the worlds,
A silent love they have
made...

Request For Assistance

I must find it.
I must.
I've lost it,
and I have to find it.
I can't go on without it.
But I can't seem to find
it.
Can you help me?
Have you seen it any-
where?
Oh, m, you haven't?
I've got to find it.
Can't stop till it's found.
My, my, I've lost my
mind
and I can't seem to find
it.

The Sacrifice

I did it.
I said I would if I had to,
and I did.
I made a promise.
and I made the sacrifice.
I did what I had to do for
the child.
It is a very special child,
a child who can save
everyone.
The child has a lot of
power,
but still I made the sac-
rifice.
She wasn't quite ready
yet.
I was sent to protect her,
and now I'm gone.
Gone from the world
that I was in.
I know that someday,
when the child is strong,
I'm sure she'll bring me
back.
I'm not dead, not really.
I still have a body,
I'm just in an altered
state of being.
The child will bring me
home,
yes, when she can.

She loves me for making
the sacrifice.
but if she can never
bring me back,
that is okay, too.
I did choose for myself
to make the sacrifice.

The Heart of Inno-
cence

Time slips past us all,
and we become what we
were destined to be.
In the darkness of the
deepest and most hope-
less and desperate night,
I've learned the praise of
what I have to be happy
for in this world.
When it is all gone and
all is wrong, you fight a
desperate fight.

It is a horror beyond any
that may be seen in this
entire world
to watch your friends
die before your very eyes
and fade away.
It is like cutting your
own heart from your
very chest to see
all that you've loved and
cherished taken from
you, what can I say.

Love is a strange thing,
and it makes people do
things that they would
not.

Love can make a man
choose a path of unre-
deemable evil for
the reason that he will
die and his lover will live
on without him.
The choice is made with
love in mind, but to evil
it opens the door.

I cannot hate. It is not in
my heart to hate anyone
or anything,
not even those who have
brought me hurt and
pain and harm.
I feel keenly pity for this
creature that was once a
man and loved,
like we all do at one time,
and fell under an elven
woman's charm.

It is hard for us to un-
derstand and it is hard
for us to even think of,
but something so horri-
ble, and evil beyond all
hope and aid
could have once been a
great and regal king of
times long past.
Sometimes there are
choices, and the wrong
ones that are made.

I ask you not to do any-
thing that you would
not normally do.
I ask you not to spare
the creature that has
brought me so much
pain.
I ask you to understand
that sometimes there is a
good soul
that takes the wrong
path and many among
you would do the same.

You ask how I can say
this, after the torture
I've been through,
and all I can say is that
my heart beats within
me good and true
and I cannot make
things different by hat-
ing those that have
hurt me so deeply as this
man, but I have nothing
that I may do.

Dead Cold

There used to be light in
my eyes.
Then it was stole by the
lies.
And it all dies.

Dark and black,
The sun is gone.
Dry and cold,
The warmth is gone.

The ground is cracked,
The rivers are barren,
Even the ocean is lacked.
And it all dies.

We have been cursed,
And it is worse than
death.
We watched it all die,
But so sad, we do not
die.
And now there's no
death,
No, not for use,
But for all else.

So very dark, so very
cold,
The sun is gone,
Oh, so very dry and

black,
So very dead.

fairy tale world

fairy tale world
in the multi-pixilated
glass
or on the silken white
with colors of life mov-
ing.
ancient tale
from long ago
a beautiful maiden
in frightful distress.
young dashing prince
comes riding
gleaming armor, white
horse
and rescues our maid
from the brink of dan-
ger.
please.
show me a maiden today
and then show me a
prince.
There are no white
horses
and armor is rusty and
encumbering.
The shining lights
tell us lies on reality.

Once a King

I was once a king.
But now,
the days and the nights
have run together
melting into one thing,
neither discernible any-
more.
These four walls are all I
know,
concrete and solid.
They would not even
give me bars.
How long have I been
here?
Days? Weeks? Months?
Years?
I know not, for I've lost
track.
Why am I here?
I would not let them
control,
so they took over.
The people are con-
trolled now.
They think me dead.
And my queen is.
One day my people will
rebel,
And then they will find
me,
dead or alive,

and will know,
I did not betray them.
I only wanted them to
be free.
True, I may never see the
daylight again,
but I did what I could
I will stay here forever,
because I was willing to
die for them,
and still am.
Locked away,
I can only hope.
And hope I will until the
moment of my death.
Yes, I was once a king...

My Legacy

I am prepared to fight.
I am armed with the
words and ideas to speak
out against them.
They are those who try
to control the will of us
all.
They are those who try
to control the will of us
all.
They are those who tell
us what to think and
feel.
I will not listen to their
words any more.
I will think of my own
words to say, I will feel
my own feelings.
I will say that we should
think and feel for our-
selves.
And there are many
other people who agree
with me.
These people and I will
fight them.
They can control us all,
but they cannot control
this idea.
I will make sure that this
idea never dies.

They can kill me, but my
legacy shall live on for-
ever.
I am willing to die for
what I believe is right,
my freedom.
We all know that we can
win this fight for free-
dom.
If we can' t win in this
generation, we will win
in the next.
And I will lead us to vic-
tory.
We will defeat those
who try to control us.
Why do I want to do all
of this?
Because   no   one's
thoughts and feelings
should be controlled,
And because I will be
controlled no longer.

Celestial Honor

Celestial entities, come
to me.
Sun and moon and stars,
oh please, come and see.

Sun, smile your smile
bright.
I honor you just past
night.
You brighten the world
with your light.
And everyone knows
your might.
Because you are high in
our sight.
Sun, smile your smile
bright.

Moon, so happy and
bright,
You show the way in the
dark night,
When all is black, you
give your light,
And tides are your only
might,
I honor my nightly
sight,
Moon, so happy and
bright.

Stars, twinkling so
bright,
Pinpricks of hope in the
night,
So very small is your
light,
I honor your small
might
When you rise within
my sight
Stars twinkling so
bright.

Oh, beauteous entities
come to me,
Sun and moon and stars,
I honor thee.

Dark and Light Intertwined

Dark and light shall intertwine,
the shadow will fall once
more,
and the visions of the
One
shall lead us all to the
door.

Dance the shadows,
dance them still,
and bind together the
two
who will grant us the
freedom
to forge the allies anew.

For the city shining great
will fall from hubris of
all
if the shining shadows
die
'fore their army stops
the fall.

Mithril touching smoke
shadow,
twining together and
find
in the hour of great need

Mithil and shadow will
bind.

Rise up, rise up, a child
no more.
Rise up, rise up a pawn
no more.
Prophetess and Knight,
bind ye both.
Tell all of them what is
in store.

Oppression

They live in a world with
little hope,
where they live each day
sick with fear.
The humble leaders
that keep them in fear,
Tell the world that
things are fine.
But the people know dif-
ferent.

They are the ones living
it.
Men jailed in the darkest
jails,
just for wanting their
freedom.
Women who have their
children
taken away to learn to
fight
and kill without ques-
tion.
Children forced to
watch
as their parents die in
shame
before their very eyes.

People dying every day
in tortuous inhumane

ways.
These are the people
who know.
They live in this world
of hurt and hate.

In silent darkness,
A woman's face is wet
with tears,
A man's heart is full of
loneliness,
A child's soul is full of
fears.

There is no fate worse.
They do what they are
told,
without objection
because they fear pun-
ishment,
these people without
freedom.

Except for those few,
those who fight,
not with weapons,
but with thoughts and
ideas.
They can be hurt.
They can be killed.
But they can't be con-
trolled.
They are quite willing to
die
for what they believe in,

their freedom.
They know that if they
die,
their legacy will live on.
They believe that they
can win.
And they can.
If not in one generation,
then in the next.
They will continue to
fight
until they win.
and they will win one
day,
because they believe
they can.

Darkness I Be

Through all that has
been,
and all that will be,
here I am to speak for
you
and here I am to make
you see.

The darkness comes
nigh to you,
but don't let the fear
grip you through.

All is not lost to the life
you lead
if you just trust in words
I say.
You will find a different
place,
and somehow it'll be
okay.

Turn you away from
me,
and look into the dark
and you will see there
more
that has come to make a
mark.

Find the light that you

seek,
find it past the dark
night.
For your light cast away
a shadow of that light.

Without your light, my
sweet,
there would be none of
me.
And you know that I am
true.
And you know what I
be.

Sent Away

I have no home any-
more.
I had to leave.
They made me go.
I left my family behind.
I left my everything be-
hind.
Such very sweet sadness,
It resides in my heart.
The tears don't come
anymore.
That well is dry.
My head is full of exalted
pain.
It was not my choice.
They said that if I left
my family would live.
Am I an exile, an out-
cast?
I guess I am.
I had a beautiful life,
but now it's all gone.
And there is not a thing
I can do.
Not now not ever again.
And I don't even know
why.

The Olden Child

The child lives.
So all people rejoice.
They were not able to
kill her.
She'll live forever,
she can't die now.
She is our only hope,
our only chance for true
survival.
Only she can fix our
broken souls.
We could not let her die.
For if she did,
so would we perish.
They tried to kill her,
and they have failed.
She will help us,
and then she will move
on.
After she saves us from
ourselves.
Yes we destroy ourselves
every day
but our eyes are closed
to it.
This child will open
them.
She looks so young and
innocent,
but look in her eyes.
You will see wisdom be-

yond her years.
She will help us learn
how to live.
And then she will help
another.

Encounter By the Hero

Wandering hero,
lost in the dark night,
cannot find your way.
You are lost in my wood.
Shall I help you find
your way?
I shall watch.
Will you hurt my wood,
crushing and crashing?
Or will you rest and
wait...
As the sun prepares to
rise,
you have slept long in
my presence.
Waking I whisper to you
directions.
You leave at dawn
headed on your way
home.
You will tell your friends
a fairy gave you the way.

In A Day

In a day, in a night,
I see him.
He processes my
dreams, my mind.
He is my best and worst
dream.
But he is not a dream.
Not really.
He loves me...too much.
He is a jealous man.
He won't allow me away
from him.
The last time I was with
a friend,
The friend is gone.
I don't know what hap-
pened,
I just know it was bad.
And he didn't visit for
weeks.
He was mad.
I haven't made him mad
since.
Lately, I've become
afraid.
He's more aggressive,
and we fight a lot.
In my dreams...
Now, I wish that he'd go
away.
He never says anything

of love any more.
He used to.
Now that time has past.
I think that he is a horri-
ble thing.
He thinks I'm his, and
only his.
I want to get away, but I
can't.
He'd kill me.
I'm sure of that.
I want him to leave...
In a day, in a night...
I still see him.

Dead Winds

The winds blew in cold
on my heart this spring,
to blow in emotions
around in red.
The air held such
a mournful sounding
ring,
the chill around me
nearly feeling dead.

I now listen, the wind
tells me of dear Joan,
sounding like the woe-
ful sound of oboes,
I will listen to the wind,
endless dark moan.
Oh so much here within
that no one knows.

I know too well the
deep, the depths of dark,
like so many songs of
those so forlorn.
I think inside me death
has left a mark
this mark that I only be-
gin to mourn.

Oh, mourn for me not
as I fade away,

and listen to what the
wind has to say.

Strange Things Happen

Strange things happen.
How do I know?
They happen all around
me.
Strange things like you
have never seen.
Because you can't.
Why can't you see them?
I do not know.
Like when you're in a
crowd calling out
And no one seems to
hear.
I once saw a child ab-
ducted
In front of at least twen-
ty people.
Not a person saw it hap-
pen,
Except for me.
Why me?
I can't tell you.
Maybe because I am dif-
ferent.
Something strange is
happening.
Somewhere as I write
this.
Now I see, the world
falling apart.

Bad things happen.
Horrible things,
And nobody knows but
me.
I wish I didn't know
this.
I wish I were not so dif-
ferent.
And how can I be so dif-
ferent?
I wish I knew.
I do know I shall soon
die.
They will make sure of
that.
They always do.
Soon it will be only
blackness for me,
Because strange things
happen...

Far From Home

I am far away from
home.
So very far.
I'll not see my home
again.
And my eyes tear a little
at the thought.
Such is my life.
The life of a woman
who has been
Sent away.
My people find me dis-
tasteful,
And, in truth,
I find them much the
same.
I do not live
Where I cannot do as I
like.
Rules, I disobeyed.
Orders, I disregarded.
And they sent me away.
Ah, well,
Now I live as I wish to,
They do not.

Conspiracy

There is a conspiracy
going on.
It is against me.
They are always doing
this to me.
I guess they don't like
me.
They are always mean to
me.
They must want me to
leave.
I won't go, won't com-
ply.
They don't realize how
smart I am.
I'm smart enough to see
through
their   transparent
schemes.
They only want to hurt
me.
I won't let them.
I can always get to safety.
But they still find me.
Why do they do this to
me?
I don't know.
Maybe they think I'm
bad.
I'm not bad.
They say I need their

help.
That's not true.
They only want to hurt
me.
I feel them.
I don't rely on my sight
much anymore.
They can trick your eyes.
I wish I could get away.
But they always find me.
There's just so much
conspiracy.
I don't know anymore...

Exile

I am an exile.
I was sent away from my
home.
Why?
I crave freedom.
I want to choose my
own life.
I loved a man,
But they said I could not
love him.
I could not love the man
they chose for me.
So I spoke out against
them.
Who is this man I see?
It is my love.
Now we are together.
Two people rebelling
against totalitarian rule.
We may live in the jun-
gles,
We may barely survive,
But we are free.
And our children will be
free.
No one will tell our
children how to live,
I may be exiled,
But I'm free.

Flight of the Pegasus

She climbs upon the
muscled back.
The plunges her hands
into the white fire that is
his mane,
And she holds on tight.
The Pegasus takes flight.
She feels the wind in her
face.
It brings a perfumed
smell that she knows is
His sweet breathe.
His wings seem to catch
the light and holds it
captive.
Setting the feathers on
fire with a mystical light.
He whinnies;
high and sweet music
that lingers on the air.
His wings beat out a
steady and true rhythm.
She laughs as he lunges
first right then left.
She is free.
She is only with Pegasus.
The mystical animal
calls out.
She feels her heart beat
faster,
Her breath comes

quicker,
Ashe begins his ascent to
the clouds.
And she smiles.
She feels amazing feel-
ings,
Her heart is filled to the
brim with love,
Her eyes are filled to the
brim with sheer joy,
As she rides on the flight
of the Pegasus.

Vortex

I dwell in a vortex.
It is a place where noth-
ing exists,
A place where every-
thing exists.
I am a person, yet I am
not.
I live, yet I do not.
It is really a place of
thought where anything
exists.
I live here and always
here.
You could come to the
vortex, if you can get
here.
Most people don't make
it because it is a hard
trip.
If you can make it, it is
wonderful.
This is a place where
thought is life.
But it is not really life.
It is really an existence, a
good existence.
There are no worries or
cares.
You just live here.
It is beautiful and won-
derful,

To hear the sounds and
see the sights,
but they aren't real.
This is a vortex of
thought.
You can hear and see and
hear what you want to.
The only problem is
getting here.
Some can make it as I
did.
We are luck.
If you can get here,
You can live in complete
peace in your thoughts.
This is the vortex I will
forever live in.
Why don't you try to get
here?
You'll never have prob-
lems again,
If you can get here...

The Need

He has a Need.
A need to kill.

If he doesn't kill, he
thinks he'll die.
He's convinced he's got
a purpose
and he can't die until
he's done.
But his purpose is only
to kill.
He is true evil.

He thrives on the blood
of the innocent
or the sound of the last
heartbeat,
and the sound of a death
rattle.
But it has to be an inno-
cent.
It has to be a pure soul.

He waits only for the in-
nocent blood.
And when he has been
fulfilled,
He waits until his need
returns.
He waits for the next in-

nocent
to befall his evil hands.

Return to the Past

If you know what to do,
If you know what's for
you,
If you think it's really
right,
If you think it's within
sight,
Return to the past.

If you think you know,
If you think you do, will
show you,
If you are strong
enough,
If you think you're
tough,
Return to the past.

If you think you can put
up with the stress,
If you can give all you
have and no less,
Return to the past.

Riding a Myth

Her eyes fall upon the
most beautiful creature
to ever live.
His is a white so bright it
is blinding.
The golden horn upon
his head
seems to glitter and glow
in the midday sun
that filters through the
leaves of the canopy
above.
She walks up to the
mythical beast.
She rubs the smooth
white beard upon his
chin.
She walks around and
strokes his back affec-
tionately.
She then pulls herself
onto his back.
He takes off and be-
gins to run through the
woods.
The wind is on her
face, and flowers are all
around her.
And the scent is beauti-
ful.
His horn clears a path

through the thickest
briars.
Her hair blows away
from her face.
He enters a beautiful
meadow,
And she is surrounded
by his kind.
She smiles as they reen-
ter the woods.
He keeps running.
She wants to stay with
him forever.
But she can't.
She will have to leave.
She came back t o see
him, but cannot stay.
She has a life she must
live.
But for now, she does
not worry about it.
Now she is riding
the unicorn, riding the
myth.

Huntress of the Night

I am the
daughter of darkness.
I am the
emissary of blackness.

From the ending
springs the black
to wash over the whole.

Flashing eyes,
dark form, idea to flesh.
From   nothingness,   I
come.

I am the
creature of the night.
I am the
huntress of the dark.

I have pleasing shape,
lovely   scent,   musical
sound,
all to lure you into com-
fort.

Come to me.
In the dark.
Come to me.
In the black.
I'll take you away.
I'll take your life.

**Pax Vobiscum
(Peace Be With You)**

*Fiat   justitia,   ruat
caelum*
was the last thing he said
to me
then   he   kissed   me
farewell.
And   my   tears   are   evi-
dence
of what has happened
now.

I do not hide them.

Pax vobiscum
was the last I said to him.

I hope it is.
For he is dead.

He only wanted justice.
Let justice be done
though the heavens may
fall,
his last words to me
and his kiss farewell.

I'll not see him again
until I finish his task
and stand beside him
in the heavens above.

He waits for me,
and I will not make him
wait long.
I must go and do what
he could not.

Jacta est alea,
the die is cast,
and once cast,
it cannot be recalled.

Ora pro nobis.
Please.

The Flight

Her eyes fall upon a
beautiful creature,
perhaps the most beau-
tiful to ever live.

He is a white that is al-
most blinding
and his fine feathered
wings are folded
upon his shining back.

She smiles and steps up
beside him,
she strokes his head
and his great wings un-
furl.
He paws the ground
with his hoof,
and throws his head
back.

She takes this as a signal
and pulls herself onto
his muscled back.

And he takes flight.

He flies higher and
higher
and further and further
away.

She is truly free
for the first time ever.

Underneath her timid
legs
she feels the immense
and powerful
rippling muscles of his
back.

She will not fall,
He will not let her.
Together they will meet
the horizon.

Vision of Darkness

Heart of darkness,
beating within my chest.
I am the poison
that blackens the earth.
Where I step,
the ground dies.
Nothing may live.
I am a vision of dark-
ness.

Place of Fire

Into the night, he rides,
To the place of fire he
goes,
Where at dawn he will
die,
Oh, but that, this man
surely knows.

The   dragon   waits
tonight,
His breath hot and full
of fire,
To kill this young one
dead,
Just as he did to his sire.

Young knight,
Where do you go?
To fight?
Heart full with woe.

He   approaches   the
dragon's cave,
Ready to stand and to
give his life,
To follow his father
through hell,
He'll commence in the
ancient strife.

You   took   with   you,

brave knight,
Your lady's very heart,
And when you die
tonight
You will tear her apart.

Dear knight,
Turn away please.
Dear knight,
Turn away now.

Before it is too late.

What Makes Me Me

Take me
and rip me open
with nails sharp
with fearfulness.
So that you can see
what makes me
Me.

Take me
and find my center
with tools dulled
with arrogance.
So that you can see
what makes me
Me.

Take me
and dissect my heart
with knives sharp
with enmity.
So that you can see
what makes me
Me.

Take me
and fondle my tears
with hands cold
with ignorance.
So that you can see
what makes me
Me.

Take me
and locate my soul
with eyes blind
with perplexity.
So that you can see
what makes me
Me.

Circle of Stones

The sun sets fire to the
velvet dark
and pierces through the
stones tall before me.
It deepens as it reaches
mine own heart
and sets alight to my
soul as I see.
I step forward into
where I should be
in the inside, in the circle
of all.
There descends a calm
and I fall upon knee
there on the green under
stones ever tall.
I shake to my core; I an-
swer mother's call,
standing in the new-
found warmth of light.
The sun spreads its gen-
tle touch like a shroud
over me chasing away all
traces of night.
I am maiden, mother
and I am crone
and I will exist here as
one with stone...

Xanther

Evil.
It lives inside Xanther.
Who is he?
I don't know, but you
will.
This man, this Xanther,
wasn't evil, but now he
has turned.
What happened?
He changed.
He stopped caring and
loving,
and the evil took him
over.
He is not really human
any more.
Once the evil has taken
you over,
There is nothing to do
except watch.
Xanther, such is his
name that holds fear,
and anger and hate.
If only he'd cared
enough,
the evil wouldn't have
taken him over.
People like him are to be
pitied.
I think it is a pity,
all those lives wasted to

evil.
But I'm using Xanther
as an example.
Please, if you care about
yourself
and the people around
you,
don't turn to the
hate...to the evil.

Overdrive

Faster.
Must go faster.
Must go fast as possible,
And even them,
Must reach overdrive.
If it is not possible,
Then it will be too late.
Must do it,
Because you just have to.
It is important.
You   must   reach   the
highest speed,
Or die.
That's why.
And why is that, why
death?
It is unknown.
Losing speed...
Not in overdrive...
Must   go   into   over-
drive...
One...getting ready...
T w o … . b r e a t h e
in...breathe out...
Three....buckle in...
Four...stretch out...
Five...deep breath...
Six...quick   look   be-
hind...
Seven...check   both
buckles...

Eight...switch on over-
drive...
Nine...finger on the red
button...
Ten...press the red but-
ton...
Button flashes.
Lights turn red.
Ready, set, go,
Overdrive.

Healing Bath

Here she is not ever al-
lowed to be
though here she hides,
she is watching tonight
as all the men bathe in
the dim torchlight,
nude in the warm water
that is the key.
Waters bubble as they
leave, hiding she
waits until they are
gone, holding her tight
to her chest for a while
more; she moves slight
and sure onto the stone
down to her knee.
She slides down clothed
into the warm green
with the sick and weak
child of her own heart
enwrapped in her shak-
ing arms, her eyes dull.
She waits, her breath
held for a time, ears keen
for interlopers to their
healing part
done, then she looks
down at eyes, now
bright, full.

Shadow Walker

Into the shadows of the
world, I creep.
Into the dark depths of
the world, I seep.

My soul is of the shadow
touched,
but it's in no way such a
blight.
My heart is tainted by
the shade
and so I know the dark
and light.

The divine hand chills
my whole soul
as I attempt to walk for
you.
My feet find the path of
shadow,
my heart and soul reach
out anew.

Keep watch on my steps
on this path
as I tread to the perfect
end.
Divinity calls to my be-
ing
and I receive that which
will mend.

I must embrace the dark
within
for the dark places will
teach me.
The dark that lies inside
my heart,
and now the dark that I
can see.

I must embrace the light
within
for the light places will
teach me.
The light that lies inside
my heart,
and now the light that I
can see.

Without the dark in this
world
there would be no light
to exist,
one must remember this
fact,
one for the other to per-
sist.

Such is the path that I
shall walk,
my feet down upon the
very line
that parts the seas of
dark and light
and this shadowed walk

shall be mine.

I walk the border be-
tween them.
Upon my right falls a
golden glow.
Upon my left falls a hid-
den dark.
And all around, the
shadows flow.

Into the between of the
world, I bend.
Into the softness of the
world, I blend.

Red Rune

Red and rich,
the roiling thunder re-
sounds
in my random thoughts.

The lightning flashes
outside,
and I see red behind my
eyes.

Time for the first light
to begin.

Rare and revered I be-
come,
a raised dais before my
right hand,
and in the rising red sun,
the rune cracks.

Running with blood,
the stone bleeds red,
and then
the rampage begins.

Save me?
Or slay me?

Only the red rune that
resounds

will reveal the reaches of
the Ronin.

A Silver Sun

In a world not far away,
where no yellow sun
or silver moon
rises above the horizon,
a silver sun
and golden moon
rises instead.
As I watch this new
world,
I wonder,
what else changed?

Breath of Fantasy

Breathe in the air
around you
and within it you will
find something
special and enduring.
Breathe out the air
within you
and within it you will
find something
precious and lovely.

Creativity and expres-
sion,
is itself the breath of
fantasy.

Sweeping the Signal

Touching the shadows
of the end,
I reached out into the
very beginning.
Shadows sweet shadows
like an infinite loop,
from beginning to end,
and in a second I could
see it all.
I swept it all away,
all the shadows,
all the light,
and then I awoke alone.
Swept away,
into the night.

Truth Within the Lie

As she spoke,
he knew what would
come.
She was real,
she said,
but he knew it was a lie.
She swore that she was
real.
But he saw the lie for the
truth.
She was not real,
except to his own eyes.
He reached out and
touched
nothing
yet everything.
And decided that this,
this lie,
was more than any
truth.

The Sun's Lover

He stood below a rising
sun.
His only desire was to be
within
the fires of his heart.
The flames were so close
and yet so very far away.

For a second,
as he felt the heat,
he thought he could see
within the brightness of
the flames
the form of a woman.
The beauty seared his
eyes
and he was blinded.

He was forever happy.

PART TWO

Whispered Reality

The world's reality can be harsh at times. Love, pain, and death all ground us in this place that is all too real. Sometimes, the reality of life can seem to eclipse the fantasies and dreams that we try so hard to hold within our fleeting grasp. Reality, however, is not dull and lifeless. The world is full of enigmas, and through creativity and imagination, fantasy can become reality.

But what makes reality? This essential question hounds us throughout our days. We accuse those who live in a fantasy of not being grounded in reality, but this is usually the idea that reality is boring and dull—the mundane day-to-day grind. We wake up, go to work, come home, eat, go to bed, rinse, and repeat ad infinitum. Does it have to be that way? Does reality consist only of what we steep in? Is there something beyond that?

Pain, death, love, fear—all of these real emotions drive us as humans. Pain and suffering aren't bad things; they mean that we have felt happiness and joy and know the difference. If there were no sadness, how could we know joy?

The same is said of life and death. Death concludes life, but it is an integral part of the cycle. We die, we are born, we live, we move on. Life's cycle cannot be stopped. Creation, destruction, and the passage of time affect us all.

So here, please enjoy a journey into some more concrete ideas than the arena of fantasy. Perhaps you will find a sliver of hope or love to take with you from here, or perhaps you will find an idea you've never thought about.

Parting in the Dark

Deep into the depths of
hell,
I will follow thee.
Till I hear the tolling
bell,
I will follow thee.

I carry in my very soul,
a little piece of your
heart,
so that I may find you,
should you and I ever
part.

Take me into your silent
arms,
One final time and all is
fine.
And before I go, you
must know,
Always I'm yours and
you are mine.

Now, I slip away into the
dark,
Will you follow me?
I know in your heart I
made my mark,
Will you follow me?

A World's Cure

The world is mad.
The world is crazy.
People are insane.
Am I the only sane one?
Who else sees how mad
it is?
I hate this place.
Am I the only one who
does?
Everyone else thinks it's
fine.
They all love their lives.
Their money and their
things.
They are all so happy.
I know what is happen-
ing.
And they haven't got a
clue.
People kill each other
Out of pure hate.
Why do they hate?
It is very strange.
Murder and thievery.
Crime with no reason.
Why do I stay here?
There is no other place
for me.
I wish there was.
How does one stay alive?
People drop bombs

Meant to kill millions.
So insane.
They could be killing
the next
Edison or Einstein.
They could kill a prodi-
gy,
Meant to cure the
world,
And it needs a cure..
This sick world needs a
cure.
For there is an almost
incurable illness
In this world of ours.

No Bond Left

So the rains have come
and so have the patter-
ings of
betrayals.

What can be done but
weep for the loss
of so much?

When the world looks
down
and you see that it is
falling
upon your head
how do you stop it?
how do you end it?

Or do you let it come
and let the pain
fall upon you
in a rain...

Such is the way of things
when trusts are broken
and family betrays.

Sometimes
there is no bond left
to break.

Turn Me Away

Turn me away
heart bleeding
cut with razor sharp
pain.

Turn me away
soul weeping
pierced with pricking
sharp
hurt.

Turn me away
spirit torn
ripped with unknowing
strong
anguish.

Turn me away
mind confused
muddled with numbing
silent
thoughts.

Turn me away
body exhausted
worn out with retched
cursed
sobs.

Turn me away
and let me go.

Love's Grip

Love holds me in a grip
that I cannot escape.
A grip that makes me cry
because it aches too
much.
The ache permeates me
and feels so good to my
tortured soul.

Blue Combined with Red

It can be light and airy.
It can be rich and dark.
It is like my moods.
It is royal or like a fresh
breeze.
It does not assail the
senses
Like some others.
It is more like being than
anything else.
It soothes my soul
And quiets the furies
within
to release the muse.

In Memory

The pain that follows
the tidings of death
doesn't leave all at once.
Time takes it away
piece by tiny piece.
And after days, months
and years,
most of the hurt and
pain is gone.
But one piece never
goes.
It is a pain deep down in
the heart
that really isn't pain,
but a kind of hope,
a kind of eternal love
that can never die.
This spark that is left
is simply what we call
memory.
And it is that one spark
that is never taken by
time.

A Mother's Thoughts

Life begins in an instant,
a touch
a kiss
and a bursting of life.

And within my body
a soul is formed
in a way that makes me
wonder
how can I question my
purpose?
For here it is...

Touch the future
within yourself
and maybe you'll see
or maybe you'll be
blinded
for it is not to be known
by those same
mothers.

Life begins anew
and two hearts beat,
one calm
and one fast
as things begin to ready
for new life
to be born.

Why Am I About to Die?

Oh, dear God above,
Please listen as I pray,
With my heart full of
love.

I was a good girl, I did
not drink.
The others did, so they
could not drive.
So I drove, but how our
plans did sink
For I wanted us all home
alive.

They trusted me be-
cause I drive so well,
And I've been driving
my car for so long
I was so careful not to
drive too fast.
Tell me, how on earth
could I tell?
How could I have
known it would all go
wrong?
How could I have
guessed our lives would
not last?

I didn't know that he

would cross that line,
I didn't know that he'd
been drinking all night,
I didn't know he would
kill me and mine,
I didn't know; soon fad-
ed would be our light...

Oh, dear God, why oh
why,
When I was such a good
girl,
Am I lying here about to
die?

Darkness

Her eyes open.
She sees only darkness.
Her eyes close.
There is no reason for
them to open.
Where is she?
She knows.
But she does not want to
accept the truth.
The truth is she is dead,
deceased, gone.
She is in the darkness.
The utter, total dark-
ness.
She is there all the time.
She is not in a needless
existence,
Though some might feel
that way.
She is simply dead.
Secretly, she has wanted
this,
The darkness, the quiet,
the time with no dis-
tractions.
She does not think of it
as being dead.
Just as resting or sleep-
ing.
Until she can wake once
more.

She can't accept that she
is dead.
But she is dead.
What is it?
Death and darkness.
She does not know how
she reached the dark-
ness,
But she knows that she is
in the darkness.
Now she lives and will
forever live in the dark-
ness.

ten thousand words

In my heart
there are ten thousand
words
that to you I could
speak.
Ten thousand reasons
to not let you go.
Ten thousand reasons
to make you stay.

I could say ten thousand
things...
I will miss you.
I will cry for you.
I won't be the same
without you.
I can't think of being
without you.

everything.

I will miss ten thousand
things...
all the plans that were
made,
all the love that we
shared,

everything.

I have found in you ten

thousand things...

a friend for someone
who is so lonesome
sometimes,
a path to the stars that I
knew was there,

everything.

Ten thousand reasons
to let you go.
Ten thousand reasons
to not make you stay.

In my heart
there are ten thousand
words
that to you I could
speak.

All of those words
lead to love.

My Future

My eyes are set.
I am looking straight
ahead,
To my future.
So close at times,
Yet so far away.
Sometimes,
It feels like I can reach
out and touch it.
Other times,
It seems a million miles
away.
Sometimes I glance back
into the past.
I see all the mistakes that
others have made,
And I say,
I will not make those
mistakes.
And yet in my heart,
I know I will make them
for myself.
I will live through all of
those mistakes,
And I will learn from
them.
As I look ahead,
I catch a glimpse of my
future.
I want to reach out and
embrace it.

But I am a little afraid of
it.
I am afraid of the un-
known in my future,
But I go on.
My future may be a bit
blurred from here,
But one day it will be-
come clear.
I will bravely go into my
future.
I am ready for what will
come.
I am ready for my fu-
ture.

Life's Children

Mother Earth.
She is life.
She gives life.
Her breath is the ocean
waves
and the winds across the
land.
Her eyes are the heaven-
ly stars
and the rocks across the
land.
He heart is in each of us.
We are her,
She is life.

Window to the Past

Tell the world to speak
nothing for a time,
whisper to it, be quiet as
a mouse,
and close your eyes soft-
ly and I'll close mine,
now listen to the past
speak in this house.
There is such noise
around us now today,
we must stop quiet in
this place and hear
because there was a time
when they would say
things upon a stage like
that without fear.
As the cold wind blows
through and the rain
pours
just think what they did
in a place like this
as people stood and
watched, chilled to a
core,|
just to view that ever-ro-
mantic kiss...
As we sit here and won-
der on the past,
remember that memo-
ries alone last.

Rather Die

She won't lose him
again.
Not after the last time.
She just couldn't take
that.
That would be too
much.
She would
rather die.
But he is forbidden.
She will love him any-
way.
And he will love her.
Everyone scorns her for
loving him.
But she cares not for
what they think.
She'll love him anyway.
She has to.

Now she finds that he is
already gone.
No! It is not possible.
After all she's gone
through to love him,
And now he's gone.
She just can't lose him
twice.
But she has.

And this time forever.

And while she lives, she
cannot love him.
Because he is gone.
This is too much for her,
She can't live without
him,
she'd rather die.
She can't love him while
she lives,
It will kill her to be
without him.
She is sure she'll die
without him.
And what she is sure of
will happen
Because she will make it
happen,
if she has to.

If she cannot have him
she would
rather die.

Sisters and Brothers

I am dying in the arms of
a sister,
Though not of my
blood,
Of honor.

I still can't believe I'm
dying.
I know who did this
We all do.

All of us know
Who knifed the fatal
blow
Now that my sister
knows.

There is only one justice.
The guilty will be pun-
ished
They killed me.

And my brothers and
sisters will make them
pay.
A brother beside me
kneels...

"Vengeance shall be
yours,"
I whisper touching his

face.

As my life slips away,
I feel the pressure of his
lips on mine,
And the vibration of the
last words I will hear,
"Vengeance is mine,
the guilty shall be pun-
ished..."

Time of Dying

Time to know
what fear is,
what horror is,
what pain is,
what grace is,
what love is,
what life is,
time to die.

The Wounded

She has been wounded.
Her heart was pierced by
cupid's arrow.
When her heart was
shattered by the poison
words.
Broken pieced to be
scattered by the whis-
pering wind.

Love was once sheltered
in to pieced scattered by
the whispering wind.
Once her heart was filled
with life and love.
Now her heart is bro-
ken.
She can love anymore, at
least, not yet.
For fear of those
scattered pieces being
crushed.
She tries to pick up
the pieces and put them
back together.
She wants to try to love,
But it is so hard to do.
She is still filled with
pain
from the last time she
took a chance.

She can't even think of
trying it again.
To her it is something
she can do without.
Or so she thinks.
What she doesn't know
yet is
that there is no life with-
out love.

She doesn't want to
dare,
Though she longs for
her heart to beat with-
out pain.
But how?
And have her heart shat-
tered again?
A person at a total loss is
what she is...
What should she do?
Why doesn't she know?
Because she is one of the
wounded.
Another of the poor
souls trying to find
the will to pick them-
selves back up.

Death

Death.
What is it?
The shutdown of all life
functions.
But is that really true?
Not really.

Is it also the shutdown
of the spirit, heart, or
soul?
You can't mend a bro-
ken spirit.
You can't piece together
a heart.
You can't fill an empty
soul.

If your spirit is broken,
If your heart is shat-
tered,
If your soul is empty,
You can't survive.

If your spirit is unbro-
ken,
If your heart is whole,
If you soul is full,
You can survive,
Long after your body
dies..

Do not go wrong, do
not give in.
Don't let your spirit be
broken,
Don't let your heart be
shattered,
Don't let your soul be
emptied,
Because if you do,
There is no turning
back,
There is only death.

Simone's Eyes

The eyes.
I'll never forget the eyes.
Oh, God, I'll never for-
get her eyes.
Pleading until the last.
My hands tried to hold
on tight,
But she slipped away.
The blood rushed out
through my fingers.
There was only a flash of
light,
And a resounding echo.
Sending another girl to
young to die away.
Sent too early to her
tomb.
I tried to hold on to her
But she left this world.
And her name was Si-
mone.
One day I may forget
that name,
But I'll never forget her
eyes.
So many plans,
Blown away in the
night,
Whisked away on a bul-
let,
A vengeful bullet for

another.
Sorrowful death,
Dying in my arms
I couldn't save her.
She didn't blame me,
She thanked me for try-
ing.
And at the end,
I saw something.
A peace, a hope, a love of
some kind.
I hope to see that for
myself one day.
But only if I can save
myself first.

Take My Hand

I'm reaching out to you.
Take my hand.
I'll pull you up.
I'll hold you in my arms,
so safe and warm.
I'll chase away the fear.
I'll keep away the night.
I'll kiss way the pain.
I'll love away the fright.
There will be no one
who will hurt you again.
There will be no one
who will make you cry
again.
In the sweet, velvet dark,
lay your tears upon my
cheek.
In the dark, lay upon my
breast,
like a child ever so meek.
Let out all of your tears,
Let out all of your fears.
I'll hold you so tight,
until   the   daylight
breaks,
and the dark is gone,
and so are the shakes.
I give you all my love
I will take you above
all the pain you've ever
known.

I'll give you love you've
never been shown.
All you have to do,
is take my hand.

The White Ferry

The dove has come
to ferry my soul
up to heaven.
The dove is pure
and white
and clean,
just as my soul is
as I ask
upon my last breath
for final forgiveness.

Inflicting Judgments

'Tis written,
"Judge not, lest ye be
judged."

Do you take me for the
fool?
You, one who does not
obey a simple rule?

But you judge me.
Do you not see?

I don't dress right,
So you smile and say its
fine
In your head you tear it
apart
Behind my back,
With all your might
You seem to hate all that
is mine
You judge me, it hurts
my heart.
Behind my back.

You look at me,
And you don't even see.

Does it matter what I
wear?
Does it matter how I

look?
Does it matter what I
have?
Does it matter what I
do?
It's too much for me to
bear.

With hurt at you I have
shook
For my wound there is
no salve,
You hurt my heart, and
you know.

Pleasure and Pain

Pleasure.
When you are with me.
When you love me.
When you kiss me.
When you leave.
Pain.
When you are away
from me.
When you hurt me.
When you hit me.
When you come back.

One Night in Time

A night in time.
A heart left alone by an-
other.
The other heart cared
not.
A tear falls in silence,
leaving only a broken
heart
untended after so long.
No love is in the other,
not any more.
It left long ago.
No capacity for love
anymore.
Unable to understand
the pain
This heart feels,
the other goes on its way,
not knowing.
Then this other,
looks back once or
twice,
and sees the pain,
this night in time.
This one weeps in the
night.
The other begins to re-
turn.
But turns its head away.
And the other heart
runs fast away.

Not wanting to see
the pain it caused the
other,
running faster away.
But still looks back
to see silent weeping of
this heart.
Pain springs in its own
heart.
Tears come
but this other heart only
runs faster.
Afraid it really loves this
one.
Scared beyond belief
as this one watches
silently,
on this night in time.

Interface

You've got to interface
with the world.
The interface between
Us and nature and us
and machines and be-
tween each other.
Anytime, anywhere.
You have to interface.
In time, we all learn no
interface.
We soon don't realize we
do.
We go through our lives
and we interface.
Going about our lives
not realizing what we
do.
What we do and harm.
What do we do to harm?
In so many ways and we
don't even know it.
We are blinded from
these things.
We are taught not to
take notice.
But if you forget what
you are taught,
Your eyes will open, and
you will see
How we often harm
with this interface.

It's clear how wrong we
are.
We destroy, we anni-
hilate and don't even
know it.
We don't it by be-
ing here, by doing any-
thing...
We don't know...or do
we?

School Girl

From the time of birth,
There is money for col-
lege.
As soon as the concep-
tion,
there is the expectation.

Associates, bachelors,
masters, doctorates!
Degree, degree, degree!
Take up the chant, girl
child!

Kindergarten,
Little girls must do well,
for the degree.
Elementary,
Good girls must learn,
for the degree.
Middle School,
Young ladies must re-
member, for the degree.
High School,
Young women must get
the grades, for the de-
gree.

Graduation,
Pick your destiny,
University, College or
Vocation.

Prepare, girl child!
Take the trip down the
aisle.
Make way for a woman
in training.

Women must succeed!
We'll show them we can.
Girl child prepare!

Take your only free
breath.
Now get ready!
Girls must learn that
women must roar!
To roar, you must have
the degree!

Smothered in books,
Just to learn to roar.

Lone Heart

A single tear.
Just a single tear.
One. No more. No less.
It slips silently down her
face.
Silently, in the darkness.
Where there was once
two heartbeats,
There is no one.
There were two lives,
Now there is only one.
The other has been ex-
tinguished,
In the blink of an eye,
A weeping eye.
In that span of time.
The heart that sill beats
Holds so much sorrow
For the one she lost.
And hate.
Hate for that which
killed the other heart.
In the lonely room.
This heart once loved
another,
But now that heart has
quit beating.
The blood stopped
flowing
Through the stilled
veins.

The heart that is left to
live
Without the other,
Cries but one tear.
One is all that is left to
shed.
This life has lost the
meaning.
The reason it remains is
simply revenge.
Upon the one who sep-
arated these two hearts.
Then this lone heart
Can finally join the oth-
er.
In death as in life, to-
gether forever.

Likelihood

It's likely that they
didn't mean to.
It's likely not their fault.
In all likelihood every-
thing's fine.
Doesn't matter much.
I'm dead and innocent,
And they killed me,
Yet are alive and guilty.

On Marriage

What is marriage?
To me it should be
the intertwining of
souls,
not a piece of paper
or even a preacher to say
in sight of God I am
wed.
God already knows.
Why do paper and
words
mean more than souls?
In this era of divorce
that paper is really
meaningless
as are those words.
I have found my soul
mate,
something so true.
Why do I need a
piece of paper to show
it?

Letting Go

Time to say good-bye,
Time to give final
farewell,
To a friend who's gone.
Whether a close friend,
or a friend not even
know yet,
it is time to let go.
Say good-bye not with a
heart
laden with pain and
grief
at being left behind.
But say farewell with a
heart
that is lit with the light
of love
at being left behind.
Forget all the hurt,
And remember the love.
And say good-bye and
farewell
without tears at being
left behind,
but with happiness at
the love
that friend left behind
for you.

Angel's Face

The rain fell down
The lightning flashed
If only I'd known
The thunder crashed.

He was driving much
too fast,
had been drinking much
too long.
How could we have
known that the last
Thing she'd hear would
be a song.

Smiles full of eternal
love,
they passed between us
that night.
As rain down poured
from above,
I knew not I'd lose my
light.

We came around a dark
curve
and then his lights, they
blinded me.
Then sounds came that
broke my nerve,
then I was unable to see.

I heard her sweet voice,
an angel's sigh,
and then I knew that all
was to end.
For my love, my angel,
was to die
Angel, your wings to me
will you lend?

I then touched her sweet
angel's face
and looked deep into her
dark eyes,
able to see, roses and lace
And an angel in the
darkness dies...

Fly to heaven, sweet an-
gel,
I'll be good, and I'll meet
you there.
Oh, sing with them,
sweet angel,
I'll be along my angel
fair.

So in my arms she closed
her sweet lights,
And then she slipped so
very far away.
For me there are many
empty nights,
I'll see my sweet angel
again, one day.

Very Wrong

Something's wrong,
When a child ODs.
Something's wrong,
When you look straight
through me.
Something's wrong,
When people kill over a
word.
Something's wrong,
When people fight over
things most absurd.
Something's wrong,
When you can look at
me and lie.
Something's wrong,
When you're always
high.
Something's wrong,
When your best friend is
dead.
Something's wrong,
When they died for
what was said.
Something's wrong,
When this lasts so long.
Something's wrong.
Yes, it's very wrong.

Like a Child

Let me come to you
in the night, in the dark,
Let me feel brand new
in the night, in the dark.

Let me curl up in your
arms,
like a child, a little child
Let me hide from life's
harms,
like a child a little child.

Let me cry long and
hard there,
in your arms your strong
arms
Let me let it all go with-
out care,
in your arms, your gen-
tle arms.

Second Chances

In life,
There are no second
chances.
You get one chance at
everything.
You get your shot.
You don't get two.
After your chance is
past,
There is no other.
Your chance comes and
goes in one fleeting sec-
ond.
There aren't any other
chances.
When you take your
chance,
You should try to make
the right choices,
Because you can't
choose again.
If you choose wrong,
You must face the con-
sequences.
If you choose right,
You make take the re-
wards.
It's all just a wheel of
chance.
Only, you only get one
spin at a time.

You can spin the wheel
with all your might,
But it's all just a chance.
Spin the wheel.
Round and round it
goes,
Where it stops,
Nobody knows.
It is a wheel of chance
with one spin.
That one chance, that
one stop on the wheel
that leaves no turning
back.

The One

Take my hand,
Lead me into your heart,
Teach me to love,
And I'll be yours forev-
er.
Don't let me go,
'Cause I fear I might fall.
And if I fall,
Don't leave me alone,
that's all I ask.
Don't make me cry,
and I will love only you.
Don't hurt me,
and I will be with you
my whole life through.
One man, one hope, one
love,
that's what I want...
and I want it to be you.

Shades

Shades of many colors.
Passion in a flash of red.
Sadness in the midnight
of blue.
Love in an off shade of
pink.
Calm in a deep well of
purple.
Happiness in a glimpse
of yellow.
Envy in a strip of green.
Serenity in a splash of
white.
Adventure in a dollop of
orange.
Death in the depth of
black.
Shades of color,
They affect our lives.
They are our very life.
Not just mine or yours,
The very life of the en-
tire world.
These colors, there are
so many,
These beautiful colors,
Represent all we are,
And all we shall become.
Colors of the world and
of emotion.
They will live after we

die.
Brilliant colors,
shine on a bright day or
moonlit night.
So many shades of color.
So many shades of emo-
tion.
Both flow with the
stroke of a brush.

The Cloud

The clouds I see
above me fly free.
Where I am, all alone
One catches my eye,
as it, slow, flies by.
Ah, how the sun shown.
Oh, to be up there,
In weather so fair.
I would love to fly free.
Upon this cloud I would
go.
If to fly, how I did know,
with this cloud I would
be.
Floating   above   the
world so high,
with a love that can nev-
er die.
The feelings, oh, so true.
It has gone, that lovely
cloud.
There's no more to say
out loud.
I wish to fly, I do,
up with the clouds, so
free.
That's where I want to
be.

Time To Go

The man comes in.
I know why he's here.
I wish he'd leave me
alone,
for just another few
minutes.
Just a few.
I want to stay here an-
other little while.
He says it is time to go,
and so it is.
Time for me to die.
I stand and go.
It is too late now
for what I would do.
I would live.
But now it is time to go.

Leaving the End in the Beginning

Walking through the
world
I have to wonder who is
really here?
Are they even aware that
I am alive?
Are they even aware that
they are alive?
I wonder...
I wonder...

I have to leave
I have to
I have
I

Working   my   way
through it all
back and forth I have
gone,
and instead I come back
and the beginning
is open in my hands and
I am staring at the end-
ing.

Stepping back,
I turn around,
and I know that

I
I have
I have to
I have to leave

I have to leave the end-
ing
right here
at the very beginning
before it can destroy me
entirely.

Soul of Fire

Blessed is the flame
that ignites our own fire
and opens up our soul.

Heart of Water

Blessed is the flow
that begins our own
blood
and filters our heart.

Mind of Earth

Blessed is the stone
that shakes loose our
own grounding
and secures our mind.

Spirit of Wind

Blessed is the wind
that opens our own
breathing
and frees our spirit.

Broken Ice

revulsion and spinning
hate
as the world begins to
revolve
and the bitterness be-
gins to melt.

The ice has fallen down-
ward.
And shattered like glass.
The ice has fallen down-
ward.
And shattered like glass.

reminding and spurning
love
as the world begins to
turn
and the saltiness begins
to melt.

The ice has fallen up-
ward.
And shattered like glass.
The ice has fallen up-
ward.
And shattered like glass.

envision and turning
back
as the world begins to

spin
and the hatred begins to
melt.

Crystal Standards

Dripping,
dropping,
crystalline salt water
finds its way
down into my fear.

Slipping,
stopping,
the ending of all of my
pain
is very near.

Tripping,
tropping,
the world shifts by my
broken heart
as I disappear.

Infinite

His world is not like
your world.
There are too many
things you don't see.
His world is so much
more.
And you refuse to try to
see.

My House

In my house you will
find
A broken couch.
(Too   many   times
jumped on)
Stained carpet.
(Too   much   playing
dough fallen)
Marked walls.
(Too many creative mo-
ments)
Scattered toys.
(Too much time spent
playing)

In my house you will not
find
Perfection.

And that's okay.
Because you will find
Happiness.

Imperfect Love

I never knew how im-
perfect love was.
There is pain and anger
and frustration
that I never realized was
there.
But with that imperfec-
tion
it is real.

My Sweet

I watch you each and
every day.
And I wonder how hard
your road may be.
Not fitting the world's
defined normal
makes you someone
worth getting to know.
But there are those who
judge
without taking the time.

My sweet child,
I don't wish to change
you.
I don't wish to make you
fit in.

I want the world to
change.
I want the world to ac-
cept you.

But until they do,
you will be accepted
completely
in this heart.

PART THREE

Whispered Truth?

We've reached the end, is it possible? Is it true? It depends on your definition of the truth and what you find true. As we've seen, reality and fantasy can both be true. Fantasy is what is possible, and reality is what currently is, so where does that leave truth?

Perhaps it is entirely possible that both are the truth. If possibility is the future, and reality is the present and past, then isn't the truth something more than we give it credit for? Throughout our lives, we seek the truth. We read books; we learn from teachers; we go onward and onward, and forward and forward. So the end result is the same. We discover the truth every day.

Some people believe that religion and faith are the path to truth. How can we know what's true after we pass away? So, we seek solace and truth in the arms of faith. What is scarier than the deep black unknown of what happens after we die? Faith gives us something to cling to and hold on to when we need it most. It doesn't make it right or wrong, but it makes it a part of us. Do we need to define ourselves through religion? We are obsessed with the future and our own mortality, and for us, nothing is more frightening than not knowing. Religion and faith provide us with a means to define our end, enabling us to prepare for the uncertainties in our lives.

So, is this truth that we call religion in our lives really truth? If you believe in something, it is your truth, even if it is not truth for someone else. Perhaps the biggest challenge in life is accepting that people have different definitions of truth in their lives. Living a life of truth, and being true to yourself and those around you, means accepting the idea that the word truth is extremely subjective. My truth and your truth are very different in most cases. We may share some ideas, but in the end, the question is, what is your truth?

Within this section, you will find a mixture of a lot of different poems on a lot of different topics. Their major theme is offering glimpses of life's truth. Some relate to nature, others to religion, and some to nothingness.

Good luck on this, the last leg of our journey together. Is there a piece of truth here for you? Perhaps. Hopefully, you find something to take with you.

Truth and Lies

Truth is, completely in
truth
nothing but an undis-
covered lie.

So does that mean that
All that we know are
lies?
Of course.

Even these words here
are lies.

So if everything is a lie
that means that
the   statement   that
everything is a lie
is in itself a lie.

So if truth is a lie,
does that make a lie the
truth?

Truth in lies and lies in
truth.
What is really true?
No one really knows,
and yet, that is in itself a
lie.
So there is no truth.
Only undiscovered lies.

Thoughts

My head is full of
thoughts
I cannot control.
They spill into my con-
sciousness
and rattle around
causing havoc and de-
struction
to my fragile
mind.
I fear I may explode
with too many things
inside my head.
Does it even matter
who lives and who dies?

Moment of Fear

When you sit alone,
and you know you are
not.
When you feel the pain
and you stare into the
face of it.
When there is no way
to look away.
When your eyes are wide
and your breath is quick
and your heart is a trip
hammer
in your ears.
When your legs are
weak,
your knees so like water
and a feeling in the pit of
your belly
like white-hot cold fire,
your mind races with
thoughts
too fast to comprehend.
When you see what you
can't change
and that is when you
know it is wrong.
When you feel all this
and ten times more,
you have had a moment
of true feat,
the kind that thrums

your heart
and never lets go.

Winners and Losers

Winners.
Those who have the
will.
They want to win.
They wish to only win.
They don't give up.
They will sacrifice it all.
They are the fighters.
They are the strong
ones.
They are the ones who
love.
They know what it is to
live.
They can only win.
Winners and losers.

Losers.
Those who lack the will.
They don't care.
They don't wish for
anything.
They give up easily.
They sacrifice nothing.
They don't want to be
anything.
They are the cowards.
They are the weak ones.
They are the ones who
hate.
They know nothing of

life.
They can do nothing
but lose.
Winners and losers.

That's the difference
between winners and
losers.
One is willful, the other
is not.
All people are one or the
other.
Either a winner or a los-
er.
Choose your path.
Which are you?
A winner? A loser?
Think about it...

going

I go to be going
leaving to leave
eyes shut
mouth closed
hearing not
stealthily silent
like a soft wind
sliding through the dark
this being me
so alone am I.

Knowledge

Who am I?
Who are you?
First answer this then
ask the first.
To know me
You must know you.
But you cannot know
me
since you will never
know yourself.

Speed

The speed at which
one can die
can only be described as
terrifying.
One second, warm, liv-
ing and breathing,
The next, cold, dead and
still.
Yes too fast.
But then,
would not a thousand
years be
far too fast?

Cause and Effect

Cause.
A man dies.
Two people fight.
A child is hurt.
Borders are disputed.
A man is held against his will.
The sun fades away.
Two people hold a grudge.
Drought comes upon the land.
A car speeds down a road.
Two people meet.
The sun rises.
Cause and effect.

Effect.
A leader is lost.
A friendship dies.
A tear falls.
A war begins.
A spirit is broken.
A flower dies.
A feud begins.
People die of hunger.
A crash occurs.
A love is formed.
A rosebud opens.
Cause and effect.

One leads to the other.
Anything you do is a
cause
That leads to an effect.
They are connected to-
gether.
Cause leads to effect.
The cause can be mi-
nor and the effect can be
major.
Every cause has an effect.
Sometimes its good,
sometimes its bad.
There is no way to tell
until it happens...

Tangible

The mere idea
that pain
is temporary
is quite intangible.
Rather it is temporal
and quite tangible.

Knowing Inside

Heart of fire
Or ice?
Who's to say what I am
but me?
Who's to say who I am
but me?
There is none that know
me inside.
No one can.
My heart is my secret
To reveal to whom
I'll not reveal or recall.
You cannot know me.
You know not yourself.
Turn your eyes inward
and know yourself first
before you can begin to
know
another's heart.

Into the Tomb

Take with thee,
into the deep dark tomb
the true truth.
love to hope to peace to
hope to love
always lives inside
with or without our
knowledge.

Midnight Comes

I feel it coming to me.
The fire left the sky long
ago,
and the moon rose,
turning its pockmarked
face to the world.
The earth has rolled
over,
the stars have come out.
Now i sit upon the green
grass and I wait.
I wait for midnight to
come and greet me.
Sweet darkness enfolds
my being.
A black velvet curtain is
draped on the world,
Spotted with tiny points
of infinite light.
Midnight is a sort of al-
pha and omega for me,
a birth of a new day and
the death of an old.
The bell tower chimes
the first of twelve soul
freezing chimes,
and the stars grow
brighter and the moon
grows bigger.
Twelve looming chimes,
and its gone.

The magical moment
spent.
Lasting   only   one
minute,
feeling like an eternity
for me.
Now I leave and I will
wait,
until midnight comes
around again...

     BEVERLY L. ANDERSON

First or Last

Turn to the first
and begin with the last.
Ignore the beginning
and focus on the ending.
This will lead you
full circle back to
where you began.
First and last
they stand together
so that there is no begin-
ning
or ending.
Therefore the ending
is the beginning.

Clues

See the clues.
They are everywhere.
Small and large clues.
Some are easy to see.
Some are not.
Some clues lead to more
clues.
What is the one thing
they lead to?
Don't know...
Find out.
Follow the clues to the
end.
See what they lead to.
Do so, and you may get
great rewards.
Do nothing, get noth-
ing.
Try to find the answers
to your questions.
On the way to find one
thing,
You can find the answers
to others.
The clues lead the way.
You follow the clues
every day,
As you go about your
life.
You see them and don't
know.

Clues are everywhere.
In nature, homes, work,
anywhere you go.
On vacation, in stores,
on a visit...
To see them can be easy,
If you know what to
look for.
Follow the clues down
the road of life.
You can survive easily,
If you follow the clues.

Looking

Silence.
All around.
Inside as well.
Quiet.
And alone.
Seeking peace.
And finding it so.
Like a panther
in the night.

Feline

Soft and gentle,
Sleek and loving,
Whirling, curling.
Ridged and fierce,
Spry and clawed,
Hissing growling.
Reflexes   of   coiled
spring,
Eyes of camera views.
The paw is soft,
The claw is sharp.
Satisfied purr.
Satisfied growl.
Feline and I.

Take Up Life

Turn thy eyes
away from the death
and live today
like there will never be
another like it
because there may not
be.
Ignore the ultimate end
and face the life
before you now.
Leave the fear behind
and take up life
and love.

in black and white

winds of change swirl
like scouring sands of
time
to whisk away what I
thought was right.

Was I blind to it all?
Was I seeing shades of
Gray?
When in the end...
It's all
in Black and White.

pain leaves me weak
like something has
wracked my body
because of someone's
words to me.

Seeing back through the
last years,
I've seen the changes in
those around me.
I've seen the changes in
me.
It's all
in Black and White.

when I thought I could
trust
and then found out I

could not
was when I realized it
was not right.

Now I have what is most
important,
And I don't have the pa-
tience for that
When my child comes
first.
That is why it's all
in Black and White.

Undying Life

Undying life.
What is it?
Is it living forever?
Immortality?
Or is it the soul?
Do I know?
I do not.
Do you know?
It isn't my place to an-
swer the question.
When you die, you'll
find out.
You have a heart and
soul.
You have a mind, spirit,
and body.
The body is left behind.
Do the rest go on?
To something else?
Maybe? If so, what?
I do not know.
Maybe it is better,
maybe it is worse.
We won't know until
death.
Then we see if we go on.
And only then do you
face fate.
You will face up to what
you are.
You die suddenly, we

cannot plan it.
When it happens, it
happens.
Maybe you believe there
is immortality.
I do not think so...
I think we could all be
immortal
In a different form.
But not this one, for it
dies to easy.
We will go on, one way
or another.

Price of Clarity

Eyes of clarity,
Sudden and total
And then consumed.
Vanishing in totality
from the world around.
So dear
But the price
is great.

Duality

There is a single duality,
A duality in my life.
In me.
A lover and a hater.
A friend and a foe.
A light and a dark.
A white and a black.
A good and a bad.
A smile and a sneer.
A duality.

Double but the same.
Daring and shy,
In refuge of me.
An opposite of me,
Not me, and yet, me.

One in light and one in
dark.
Honesty and deception.
It is one.
I make every choice.
And I choose them all.
I make no mistakes.
I make every mistakes.
I do it all.
In every way.
But still,
There is this duality.

Find Out

Eyes of mine, they open.
Is it my time? What is
happening?
Wait, and find out.
My hands reach out in
the dark,
My breath comes fast,
faster.
Silence fills the stillness.
Sweat beads upon my
forehead.
And I do what I
should...or do I?
I don't know,
I've never experienced
this.

Eyes of mine, they see.
And what they see...
Wait, and find out.
My heart beats so fast
and so quick,
Adrenaline rushes in my
body.
My body trembles at
the sound of another
breath.
This other breath comes
fast.
The other heart is fast,
like mine.

Eyes of mine, they know.
Who else is here?
Wait, and find out.
I see dimly the other.
I reach out in the dark
and find the other hand
As it searches for mine.
I know what to do...or
do I?
It is over in a minute.
What I have waited for
has come to pass.
What has happened that
I waited for?
Well, guess, or wait, and
find out...

The Loss

What is more precious
to you than anything?
Is it your child? Your
life? Your love?
Or maybe it's a material
thing?
If it is, I pity you.
It doesn't matter if you
lose something.
What would you do if
you lost
Your child? Your life?
Your love?
Do you know?
Have you ever thought
about it?
You would be devastat-
ed.
A child is gone in a
whisper.
A life is gone in the
twinkle of an eye.
A love is gone in a single
breath.
Have you ever felt that
pain?
It is terrible.
Imagine...
One moment you have a
child, you are living, and
you love.

The next, your child
dies, or you die, or you
love dies.
This is the ultimate loss.
The day may come
sometime.
The pain.
The loss is the reason to
shed the tears of grief...

To See

Tis a sad thing I see.
Pain and suffering are
there.
No one tries to help
these.
Can this really be?
Please,
do tell me.

Silken Stars

To sleep with the sound
of silken stars
in my sorrowed soul.
To stare up and suc-
cumb
to the sight of those
silver stars
stirring in my soul.

Aniconic Imagery

We are all endlessly icons
to be extolled by no one.
What is to become of us
when we are not sought
by anyone else
other than
ourselves?

We are nothing
but an iconic
image of an
aniconic life.

You

You-
my one and only, always
and forever my mate, my
dear,
come to me please, and
sit with me, for I do
want you near,
say what you will to me,
suave or harsh, voice on
my ear,
look to me, my life has
all before, this staring
forceful leer,
go far away please, hands
of mine, to feel the flesh
to seer,
a friend to help, this not
only you, leave me not
of that peer,
and fear.

You-
my life, to you I do un
and willful give, with
you I must share,
and me together, our
house of home, alone
wishing in our lair,
I watch by day and
night, eyes so dark
around, do really I care,

waiting for something,
alone and sitting alone,
old rocking chair,
to try love you, long ago
so long ago, I did so
hopefully dare,
alone upon me, so alone
I feel your eyes burn, this
life for not fair,
and tear.

You-
I see before, even every
single time, on each and
every day,
don't be near any more,
please leave me be, I do
want you away,
I say so and I ask to you
so, please can I want, I
cannot may,
birds are free, flying
along peaceful in air,
robin cardinal blue jay,
look down to me, voice
so much softer now, all
for me not okay,
walking out and away
too late, crimson upon
floor, I do silently lay,
and say.

You-
seem so to come, seem to
so much hate the time,

each of day do fight,
I sit alone, eyes are so
very wet and dark, to be
seeking so long in night,
to me bring, here I am to
always be, there is not a
single piece of light,
a bird I wish I was, wings
spread on high wind,
taking me into air in
flight,
eyes do flutter so very
light to me, no words
you pass by, in the sight,
breath had to come,
how these eyes are
blurred, this chest is so
tight,
and fright.

You-
I fear,
my dear, when you near,
on my ear,
you and a leer, out of
flesh to seer, with your
peer.

You-
my life you tear,
do not want to share, in
this hurtful lair, not to
care,
in my chair, I do not
want to dare, not fair.

You-
don't say,
all the day, go far away,
how can I may,
near be the blue jay, nev-
er okay, where I lay.

You-
give me such fright,
how the fight, alone I am
in night, I see no light,
need wings for flight,
not in sight, so very
tight.

You-
fear, dear, near, ear, leer,
seer, peer,
tear, share, lair, care,
chair, dare, fair,
say, day, away, may, jay,
okay, lay,
fright, fight, night, light,
flight, sight, tight.

You-
caused me all my loss.
caused me all this pain.
caused me all this fear.
caused me to go insane.
caused me all my hurt.
caused me to lie.
caused me my madness.
caused me to die.

Cosmic Child

Speak infinity,
hear eternity,
my child.

The Spider

Tis a quiet quiet time.
Black is creeping
like a spider full of ven-
om.
Should I die now?
Or wait to be bitten?

Tired

Into the abyss
I go.
It is dark,
And it is cool.
My eyes are open,
And I see naught.
There is naught to see
'Tis cool and dark
'Tis comfort to my
Tired soul.

Poisons

There are many poisons.
Poisons of all kinds.
Poisons of the mind,
body, soul, heart and
spirit.
All these lethal horrible
things.
You can die piece by
piece.
Or die all at one time.
Watch.
They are all around.
Everywhere you look.
Never forget or you just
may find out
how lethal they can be.

Time

Time comes and goes.
Time does not stop.
It knows no mercy.
It goes on no matter
what.
Time does not let you
wait.
It will not wait for you.
Don't get behind.
You can't catch up.
Not you or me or any-
one.
All times are one.
Past and present and fu-
ture.
Time is forever flowing.
Never stopping.
It is like water.

Like a river.
It carries you along.
You can drown so easily.
When you get ahead or
behind.
Stay in the present,
In the calm waters.
Time will take you in
time.
Let it.
Because,
one second,

one minute,
one hour,
one day,
one year,
one decade,
one century,
one millennium,
one infinity...
It's all the same.
It's all different.
It is time.

All Around

What is all around,
always been here,
always will be,
was here before the uni-
verse
was born,
will be here long after
the universe
is dead.
What is it?
Guess,
I'll not tell you.

The Time is Now

The time is now.
The time for what?
You might ask.
Well,
I can't tell you.
You have to find out
For yourself.
I know what time it is,
At least for me.

Tale of the Missing

Where has it gone?
Somewhere left?
Somewhere right?
missing,
missing,
where has it gone
where....
only the end
reveals
all....

A Child's Vision

Can it be so simple?
Or is it something far
more complex?
A child sees the world in
a different light,
untainted by our expe-
riences,
so perhaps if we can tru-
ly let go,
we will learn to live
with the love of a child.

The Road to Nirvana

I stopped along the
road.
There sat a young man
under a tree.
He was in quiet medita-
tion.
I moved to leave but he
spoke instead.

"How fare thee on the
road to Nirvana?"

I was confused and
asked him his meaning.
He stood slowly,
joints popping as
though he'd sat there a
while.

"Walk with me to Nir-
vana."

I did not understand
but I nodded slowly,
and down the road we
did walk.

There was silence be-
tween us.
The sun was setting in
the west,

far behind us now.
And I did not feel the
need to speak.
Soon we stopped and
the man,
his dark brown eyes
open and large,
his wide mouth parted
in a smile,
and his brown hair
blowing in a gentle
breeze,
he did speak again.

"Blessings on your way
to Nirvana."

I wanted to speak but I
could not.
He walked away from
me,
And in the distance he
was gone.
I looked down the road
ahead,
and I had peace in my
heart.
I was on the road to Nir-
vana.

He Only Said

I dreamed last night.
I stood beside a man I
knew all too well.
I looked upon him with
awe.

Are you Jesus?
My voice trembled as I
spoke.
He nodded and stared
into the beautiful sky.
So many questions.

I have to know,
What should we do
about gay people in our
world?
He smiled.
Love Thy Neighbor.

I have to know,
What should we do
about the pagan and
heathens in our world?
He nodded his head.
Love Thy Neighbor.

I have to know,
What should we do
about the bad people in
our world?

He blinked his eyes
slowly.
Love Thy Neighbor.

I have to know,
What do we do about
the poor people in our
world?
He smiled once more.
Love Thy Neighbor.

I have to know,
What do we do about
the rich and greedy in
our world?
He only said,
Love Thy Neighbor.

Silently I sat at the feet of
the Holy Son.
He gazed gently at me
and said,
You only need to do this
one thing,
And my father's king-
dom awaits.
He faded from sight.

Apple Blossoms

Blossoming in spring,
Reaching   toward   a
bright blue sky,
Breathing in sweet sun.

Apple Picking

Fruitful come summer,
Hands grasp at the pre-
cious orbs,
And the sun looks on.

Apple Leaves

Turning fall colors,
Cool breezes whisk away
leaves,
As the sun grows cold.

Apple Branches

Bare winter branches
Reach up into snow
drenched sky,
And the sun awaits.

Searching For My Savior

I went out searching to-
day,
For a cure for this bro-
ken world.
Children cry from
hunger,
And people look away.
Children go without
water,
And people look away.
Children are taught to
hate,
And people look away.
So it was, I went out
searching,
To cure this broken
world.

The hearts of men need-
ed
To be lifted up some-
how,
They needed to have
someone
That could show them
how
paramount love is,
and then I realized,
there was someone who
did this.

There was someone
who already spoke.

But people don't listen
and have forgotten.
Too wrapped up in
themselves,
They ignore the needs of
their brothers.
They ignore the cries of
the poor.
They ignore the pain of
the trampled.
Instead of listening,
They argue about right
or wrong
But always about non-
sense,
Looking away from the
truth.
Not listening to His
words.

Wasn't the savior of our
world
Already born?
1 John 4:20

I Will Be Fine

I walked outside today.
And stood upon the
back
of Mother Earth.

I wondered where we
were heading.
What will we do?
we are destroying you,
dear Mother Earth,
what will become of
you?

She spoke to me.
I will be fine.

We waste your bounty,
we ruin your waters and
forests,
we decimate your ani-
mals,
what will become of
you.

Again she spoke.
I will be fine.

How can you say that,
how will you be fine
when we are destroying
you

piece by piece?

You are not destroying
me.
You are destroying
yourselves.
I will heal in time.
Will you be here when I
have healed?
That is your choice that
you face.
Will you be here or will
you have died?
I will be fine.
You children of my
bounty,
may not be.

What is Christ Like?

I sat before my altar,
Set with candle and in-
cense.

And I spoke with
Christ.

What makes someone
Christ-like?
And do they have to
say they accept you as
Christ?

What does it mean to act
as Christ?
To be a good person,
To be a loving person,
To be a moral person,
To be a giving person,
To be an accepting per-
son,
To be a helpful person,
That is to act like Christ.
Saying you are Christ
like is not the same.

Can it be that some of
the most Christ like
Do not even follow
Christ?

In the end,
Acting as Christ would
act,
Means you have accept-
ed the word of Christ
More than vacant words
before an altar of God.

I Prayed

Last night I prayed.
And then I was an-
swered.

I prayed,
Who is right in this
world?
Christians?
Muslims?
Hindus?
Buddhists?
Pagans?
Atheists?
I prayed for an answer.
And do you know what
I received?

The divine spirit welled
in my chest.
And I knew.
It didn't matter who as
right.
All that matters is that
some
divine spirit lives in us
all,
and we are all divine.

New Life's Curse

When the burgeoning
life begins,
we know that with that
life is a curse.
There are few escapes
from curses
save death.

The curse of life which is
struggle.
Suffering and peace.
Ugliness and beauty.
Despair and hope.
Endings and begin-
nings.
Hate and love.
Death and life.

This struggle so eternal,
and this curse that fol-
lows us to the grave.
Yet it is amazing,
and awesome,
and worth every second.

Evening Shadows

Eyes wide open
as dusk begins to set in
and the stars reveal
themselves
(twinkling twinkling)
who is dreaming here
is it me or is it you
do I sleep or do I wake
and where have the stars
all gone?
(twinkling twinkling)
Eyes are shut
as dawn begins to rise
and the stars are now
hidden.

Were they ever there?

Twisted Whisper

Sweet.
Silent.
Subtle.
And it twists.

Bitter.
Boisterous.
Bracing.
And it twists.

Again.
Alone.
Asleep.
Whispers twisting.

Aware.
Able.
Awake.
Nothing there

Real Fantasy

At the end of all things,
one thing becomes real,
and that is the fantasy
that we all hold.
A dream.
A wish.
A hope.
A desire.
A want.
A need.
All are fantasies and
something that drives us
onward.
Without this drive,
there would be nothing
new.
So there is in truth,
great fantasy in our lives.

Epilogue

Whispered Shadows Between the Stars

So we've come to this, the end of all things. Well, really just the end of this book of rambling poetry that I've convinced you to pick up and read. I may know you, or you may be a complete stranger to me, but I am hoping that you enjoyed your journey through my thoughts. You may like some, and you may not like others, but I hope that a spark of wonder was lit in your heart when you perused my works.

I leave you with the hope that you will continue to journey through new and unusual poetry and literature. Sometimes, it's challenging to decide whether to read a book you're unfamiliar with or written by an unknown author and wonder if it will be a waste of your time.

Poetry isn't dead. Maybe for some people, the art is sleeping. Take a moment to stand under the stars and ponder the world beneath your feet. One of countless planets in a vast universe. Those stars, those beautiful stars, let them speak to you and whisper words of wisdom and words of poetry into your mind.

Maybe you'll never write a word about it. Maybe you'll write a book of ten poems, or twenty or a thousand. It doesn't matter. The poetry of the universe whispers deep into ourselves, and all we have to do is listen for it. It is the silence when you step outside after the first snowfall of the year. It is the rushing water when you find a river nearby. It is in the patter of rain and rumble of thunder during storm. It is in the stars and makes poets of us all.

Appendix

Hotlines and Helplines

Here you will find a listing of resources compiled by the author on the following pages. At the time of this publication, resources are considered reliable and available. Please note this may change at any time, and the authors are not liable for the content of the following groups/resources. These resources relate to events in several of my books. They may be added to or altered at any time. Local resources may be available in your area. These are only a few of the possible resources for the following needs.

Autism and Autism Self-Advocacy

Autism Self-Advocacy Network

- info@autisticadvocacy.org

- http://autisticadvocacy.org/

Autism Women's Network

- https://autismwomensnetwork.org/

Identity First Autistic

- identityfirstautistic@gmail.com

- https://www.identityfirstautistic.org

Mental Health and Mental Health Resources

National Alliance on Mental Health

- 1-800-950-6264

- http://www.nami.org/

Depression and Bipolar Support Alliance

- 1-800-826-3632

- http://www.dbsalliance.org/

National Mental Health Association

- 800-969-6642

-

Trauma/PTSD/Anxiety

Anxiety Disorders of America

- 301-231-8368

National Center for PTSD

- 802-296-5232

- https://www.ncptsd.org

National Victim Center Infolink

- 800-FYI-CALL

Eating Disorder Resources

National Eating Disorders Association

- 800-931-2237 (M-F, 11:30 am-7:30 pm EST)

- http://www.nationaleatingdisorders.org/

ANAD: National Association of Anorexia Nervosa and Associated Disorders

- 630-577-1330 (M-F,12 pm-8 pm EST)

- http://www.anad.org/

Substance Use Disorder/Addiction Assistance

Substance Abuse and Mental Health Services Administration

- 1-877-SAMHSA-7

- https://www.samhsa.gov/

AL Anon Family Groups

- 800-344-2666

- 800-356-9996

- https://alanon.org/

American Council for Drug Education

- 800-488-DRUG

- https://www.acde.org

American Council on Alcoholism

- 800-527-5344

- https://assistedrecovery.com

Harm Reduction Coalition

- 212-213-6376

- https://harmreduction.org

National Institute on Drug Abuse (NIDA)

- https://www.nid.nih.gov

Anonymous Groups

Alcoholics Anonymous

- 212-870-3400

- https://www.aa.org

Cocaine Anonymous

- 310-559-5833

- https://www.ca.org

Co-Dependence Anonymous

- 602-277-7991

- https://www.coda.org

Families Anonymous

- 800-736-9805

- https://www.familiesanonymous.org

Gamblers Anonymous

- 213-386-8789

- https://gamblersanonymous.org

Narcotics Anonymous

- 818-733-9999

- https://na.org

Sexaholics Anonymous

- 866-424-8777

- https://sa.org

Transgender Assistance and Equality

Transgender Youth Equality Foundation

- 207-478-4087

- http://www.transyouthequality.org/

Trans Student Educational Resources

- TSER@transstudent.org

- http://www.transstudent.org/

Bullying Prevention Assistance

Stopbullying.gov

- https://www.stopbullying.gov/

PACERS National Bullying Prevention Center

- 1-800-537-2237

- http://www.pacer.org/bullying/

Suicide Prevention Hotlines and Help

National Suicide Prevention Hotline

- 1-800-273-8255

- https://suicidepreventionlifeline.org/

Crisis Text Line

- Text "Start" 741-741

- http://www.crisistextline.org/

Trans Lifeline

- US: 1-877-565-8860

- Canada: 1-877-330-6366

- https://www.translifeline.org/

Suicide Prevention Resources

- http://www.sprc.org/

The American Association of Suicidology

- http://www.suicidology.org/

American Foundation of Suicide Prevention

- https://www.afsp.org/

GLBT National Youth Talk

- 1-800-246-7743 (M-F, 4pm-12 am EST/Sat, 12 pm-5

pm EST)

The Trevor Project

- 1-866-488-7386 (24/7)

- Text "Trevor" 1-202-304-1200 (F 4 pm - 8 pm EST)

- http://www.thetrevorproject.org/

Warm Ear Line

- 1-866-WARM EAR (927-6327)

- http://warmline.org/

Self-Injury Assistance

S.A.F.E. Alternatives

- 1-800-DONTCUT

- http://www.selfinjury.com/

Human-Created Disaster Helplinc

Disaster Distress Helpline

- 1-800-985-5990

- Text "TalkWithUs" 66746

Sexual Violence and Abuse Resources

National Sexual Violence Resource Center

- 1-877-739-3895

- http://www.nsvrc.org/

RAINN- Rape, Abuse, and Incest National Network

- 1-800-656-4673 (National Sexual Assault Hotline)

- https://www.rainn.org/

Domestic and Intimate Partner Violence Resources

The National Coalition Against Domestic Violence

- 303-839-1852

- http://www.ncadv.org/

The National Domestic Violence Hotline

- 1-800-799-SAFE

- http://www.thehotline.org/

The National Resource Center on Domestic Violence

- 1-800-537-2238

- http://www.nrcdv.org/

Human Trafficking Resources

National Human Trafficking Resource Center

- 1-888-373-7888

- Text BeFree (233733)

Runaway and Child Abuse Resources

National Runaway Safeline

- 1-800-RUNAWAY (786-2929) (24/7)

- http://www.1800runaway.org/

USA National Child Abuse Hotline

- 1-800-422-4453 (24/7)

National Safe Place

- Text SAFE and your current location to the number 69866 (24/7)

- http://nationalsafeplace.org/

About the Author

Beverly L. Anderson

Transgender. Bigender. Asexual. Panromantic. Kinkster. Pagan. Autistic. Polyamorous. Queer. Poet. Writer. More.

She/Her or They/Them

Beverly L. Anderson started writing at eleven, and when they did, it was apparent they would stick to something other than the every day. Her first story, written in spiral notebooks, was about a kidnapping. There were endless story ideas featuring fantastic places, monstrous creatures, and forbidden love in her mind even then. There's no surprise that these days, they favor the dark corners of the psyche over the happy and fluffy parts. Enamored with the mind, she studied extensively in psychology and related fields. She spends most of her days dreaming about stories and deciding how to make the unruly characters do as they tell them. As everyone knows, sometimes the characters take off and do what they want, no matter what the author has planned.

Beverly's other hobbies include gaming of all types, including a great love of tabletop, transgender and autism advocacy, and writing fanfiction when she can. Their interest in the BDSM community began as a simple curiosity but has led her to the road to finding a place for herself there as a Domme. She has gone on the journey of self-discovery in the last few years, finally pinning down their identity after nearly thirty years of searching. Coming out as bigender, asexual, panromantic, and polyamorous was one of the hardest things they've ever done, but it gave them the confidence to become themselves even more. An autistic person and an eclectic pagan, Beverly finds themself at odds with a lot of what society calls "normal." They don't mind, though, because they find that they are uniquely queer in every aspect of her life, and she's just fine with that.

Beverly started their writing journey seriously in 2013 when she found their way to fanfiction. She spent several years writing over three million words in various fandoms. In the last few years, they have been drawn to making those stories into original pieces and publishing them for a wider audience. Finding her publishing home helped make that dream a reality, one that they try to help others find.

Visit online: https://www.phoenixreal.net/

phoenixreal.net
Queer Love

Also by Beverly L. Anderson

Crimson Hunt - Behind the Red Part One

Kerry Graham surprises his father by coming out as gay and cross-dresser and possibly non-binary. Then again, when he starts performing in drag at a local Cabaret named The Red, where his cousin works as a tailor. He finds himself free and able to be himself in a world that has always treated him as an outcast. He's among people that understand him, and he can finally relax. At least, that's what he believes. Then, a dress arrives, seemingly an apology for a bit of bigotry from a shop clerk. No one thinks a dress can cause any harm, so he wears it under the stage lights. Things go awry, though, and Kerry wonders what could possibly be happening. A bounty hunter named Martin swoops in, convinced that he can be of aid in the situation. Along with Martin, there's an intrepid FBI agent named Zak on the trail of a pair of sadistic serial killers who target and manipulate young, attractive, feminine men like Kerry.

Kerry doesn't believe it at first. Can he be targeted by these people? Then, things start happening, and his phone and email is full of messages with horrible images of what these people plan to do to him. He's frightened but staunch in living his life. He is adamant that he won't let them win, no matter what they do to him. Still, as the manipulation and gaslighting continue from afar, he starts to doubt everything he's ever known. He begins to lose purchase on reality but finds that Martin and Zak ground him. He refuses to give in to their sadistic games, but in the end, he begins to wonder if his willpower is enough to keep these people away from him.

***

Stolen Innocence - Doctor's Training Part One

When desperate criminals find an easy target in the autistic neurosurgeon Kieran Sung, the young doctor is soon at the mercy of a local Irish mob boss with perverse desires. Despite suffering at his hands, rescue finds him with relative quickness. Pulled unwillingly into circumstances that bring his world crashing down around him and destroying the carefully laid routines and structure he desires; Kieran must find a new way to live. He discovers comfort in ways he never imagined, within sensations of pressure and binding. Taking the hand of a childhood friend who desires nothing else but to help him, Kieran realizes his heart aches for more in his life. Circumstances bind him to a tattoo artist named Varick Jaeger, an actor named Carmine DeAngelo, and a bartender named Devan Sullivan. With this unlikely trio, Kieran must learn how to handle the upheaval in a life he sees desperately needs change.

Stolen Innocence, part one of the Doctor's Training Trilogy, is a story of healing that examines D/s culture, the complexities of polyamory, and how people often deal with mental and physical trauma. Follow Kieran, Devan, Varick, Carmine, and the rest of their pack; they navigate a world that rarely accepts people who do not fit in with expectations.

***

Escaping Fate, Embracing Destiny

CJ Kim is a normal college student. He is doing what most college students do, figuring himself out, sometimes the hard way. He has some strange dreams now and then, but he just thinks they are just dreams. They're certainly nothing to worry about when reality is pressing down so hard on him. Between the demands of school and family, he has enough on his mind.

He ends up with a huge crush on a senior that is on the baseball team. He doesn't even like baseball, but he goes to games just to see him. Of course, he'll never notice a gay and nerdy English major like CJ. Things are good, though. He even has a good relationship with his parents and his twin sisters.

He never expects his family's past to come back to haunt him. It rears its head in the worst way possible and CJ finds himself the prisoner of a vengeful man. Thrust into something that goes beyond what can be considered normal, CJ finds out that there's a fate out there trying to destroy him. He doesn't know how, but he has to reach for a destiny that he can just barely see.

***

Dark and the Sword – Legacy of the Phoenix Book One

The world of Avern has moved on. It has been almost a thousand years since the day the entire pantheon disappeared. Since the Abandonment, the mortals have learned to live without gods and goddesses. The world became mundane, with little magic and even less hope. Tyrants have risen, and those able to wield what is left of magic are powerful. Forces surge in the darkness that threaten to topple the already fragile world. However, the plight of the world of Avern is not unknown, and those who watch from a distance have decided to intervene. The mortals are sleeping, however, unknowing that two great powers will soon be vying for control.

Then something happens that changes things. A young princess makes a bid for power by murdering her father. She then attempts to murder her sister, the crown princess of Lineria, Keiara. Despite a true strike aided by dark powers, Keiara doesn't die. Instead, the strike pierces the barrier between her human soul and the soul sleeping within her, the soul of the Dark Phoenix. More than a goddess, the Dark Phoenix is the legendary mother of the gods. She is a part of the Eternal Phoenix that brought life to their world eons ago, one of the primal forces of the cosmos.

***

Chasing the Silver Dragon – Part One Disconnect, Book One of the Dragon Trinity Cycle

Silver Dragon has become a bane to the werewolf community in recent years. Designer heroin, one that actually affects were creatures where normal drugs are simply a passing fancy, has infiltrated the St. Louis werewolves. One of these, a young woman named Anna Maddox, wants her brother back somehow from the brink he's standing at. To do this, she reaches out to the ancient order, the Children of Asclepius. Duncan Powell hears her plea and pledges to help her rescue her brother from the streets of St Louis.

He goes to Detective Sebastian Pearce, a member of Unit Zero, the law enforcement agency that deals with supernatural creatures that pose a threat to the peace in the world. Sebastian implores him to leave things to Unit Zero, but Duncan is stubborn and goes down to the Red District to find the young Were. Sebastian and his partner follow and then begin the mission that will either save Kacey Maddox or doom all of them.

***

Let Sparks Fly – Short Story Compilation

Romance can come from the most unexpected places. Sometimes, two people meet, and the sparks just fly between them. Then, sometimes, two people see each other every day, and don't realize the spark that exists between them.

In this volume, you will find stories of many kinds. You'll meet a pair of fellows just looking for a sub to share when they ask out two people, and a secret is revealed. A young man is pining for his very best (straight) friend when a strange entity shows him pleasures beyond imagining, along with some truth. Join a guy who secretly harbors a taboo wish he thinks will never come true. Watch the sparks as a pair of swimming rivals find themselves in a compromising position. A demon on a mountain demands a sacrifice and receives something he isn't expecting. And finally, a man finds his bliss in a woman who can completely own him.

Journey through these pages and enjoy short erotic stories of love found in some quite unusual ways.

***

Whispered Shadows – A Poetry Anthology

The twisting paths of a poet's mind lead to intriguing places, there can be little doubt of this. These places contain whispers of the writer's soul. Some paths show desired sights; others uncover unforeseen knowledge and, at times, unwanted things. The shadows conceal unknown discoveries on well-lit paths through the poet's mind. Travelers, beware: uncertain destinations await along these paths. Tread carefully. Becoming lost in the pages of the poet's thoughts may be a very real danger to these travelers.

So, come along and visit this place of shadows. Here, there be dragons, monsters, truth, and more to enjoy. Fantasy, Reality, and Truths form one hundred and fifty poems by Beverly L. Anderson. The first path is one of fantasy with mythic beasts of yore and darkness that creeps into the very bone. Fairies may fly, and dragons may soar. The second path is one of reality and perhaps questions of what is and is not within that reality. Questions of existence and what the world shows us daily are spoken here. And the final path is one of truths. These truths may be surprisingly uncomfortable or may not be the truth expected. In any case, travel the paths at your own risk.

Open these pages and see if something draws you into the whispered shadows of the very soul.

***

Reflections of the Shadow Dancer

In an abandoned dance studio, there's music and dancing unheard and unseen by anyone. The whispers in the shadows laud praises upon the figure who spins around the room, her body translucent and flickering in the night. Nothing is in motion, and yet everything moves around the room. Darkness and light intertwine and dance to cast the shadows of the world. The Shadow Dancer performs a dance that crosses the borders between the world and other surprising places within flickering shadows.

The Shadow Dancer knows the truth. Without the darkness, there can be no light. Without the light, there can be no darkness. Between them lies the shadow in which the Shadow Dancer twirls.

Enter the world of the Shadow Dancer and immerse yourself in 150 poems, living in the light, the dark, and the shadow.

COMING SOON — CHAINS OF BLOOD

From Beverly L. Anderson and J. Foster

The Chains of Blood Trilogy

Confined by Heaven – Chains of Blood Book One

The day started as any other day would. Bellamy Delacroix was shopping with his brother, and then he headed home to the inevitable discussion about his future with his mother. A woman who still cooks despite technology that doesn't require her to, his mother is an old-fashioned type in a future world.

Then, his world explodes quite literally, and he's swept up into a world beyond his imagination. A war between extraplanar creatures who call themselves angels and demons draws him in because of what he is. And what he is, no one has ever seen before—a Nephilim. He is the child of an angelic mother and a demonic father and is thus capable of channeling both the positive and negative energies of the planes. This makes him dangerous and a target for both the minions of heaven and hell.

An angel named Saniel takes him under her wing and helps him adjust as he is brought to the underground city of heaven, Elysium. He learns about what he is, who they are, and their enemies in Zion, the demons. A warning from an ally of his mother, though, rings in his head, and he wonders who he should really be trusting. Things begin to spiral in ways he doesn't understand, and the world is changing before his very eyes.

Released by Hell – Chains of Blood Book Two

Driven insane by the very people he trusted, Bellamy is caught between worlds in a way like never before. He's in the hands of Addariel, the angel both at fault for his fall from grace and the current King of Hell. His mind is only clear when he is inside his own head and his world is spinning out of control. A terrible experiment that went wrong has left him on the verge of death, and it is up to the Codex of Hell and Addariel to save him.

Then, the strangest things happen among the demons. They devote themselves to his salvation, claiming him as their mate and, more than that, dedicating the hearts they didn't know they had to him. In his madness, he captures their very souls and changes the nature of the beasts around him. Even Addariel, once only interested in power, shifts his focus to taking care of the mentally fragile Bellamy. For the first time in Zion's history, the King of Hell cares more for something other than power and conquest.

Elysium, though, is not letting go of him easily. In a misguided attempt to help him, they make a move that could destroy the fragile peace between Zion and Elysium.

Transcended by Earth – Chains of Blood Book Three

Rescuing Bellamy has become a priority for both Elysium and Zion. Adding to the mix are the Arcadians, who will stand to fight for Bellamy. Held by the angel Usiel in a location no one knows, Bellamy fights for his survival and the survival of his unborn child. Usiel wants to breed an army of angels capable of fighting demons without fearing their use of negative energy, and by doing that, he needs to rid Bellamy of the demon's child within him.

A human woman senses something off with a strange neighbor and investigates the situation. What she finds shocks her, and she knows what she must do. Taking Bellamy, unstable as he is, she flees, unsure what to do with what she thinks is a young girl pregnant with her a child her captor wishes to kill.

Meanwhile, in Arcadia, angels from Elysium and demons from Zion work together with a pirate radio station to try and find the missing Nephilim. The world is unsure, but they know they must find him before Usiel captures him again.